Daily English

조동인 저

도서출판 진 영 사

Daily English

조동인 저

2017년 11월 28일 초판 인쇄
2020년 9월 2일 초판 2쇄 발행
2021년 3월 8일 초판 3쇄 발행
발행인 박 진 영
발행처 도서출판 진영사
인천광역시 부평구 갈산동 185번지 풍진빌딩 303호
전화: 032)505-4207
팩스: 032)505-4206
E-mail: 0183734207@hanmail.net
등록: 122-91-77317

ISBN 978-89-6541-338-7 93740
값 14,000원

머 리 말

본 교재는 학생들의 일상생활에서의 영어 의사소통 능력 향상을 위해서 연구되어 쓰여졌다. 한국의 학생들은 10년 이상의 세월동안 영어 공부를 하여도 영어 의사소통 능력이 향상되지 않는 경우가 많다. 그것은 영어를 단순 암기 과목으로 생각하고 암기한 대로만 영어를 구사하려고 하기 때문이다. 이에 본 교재는 학생들이 일상생활에서 경험할 수 있는 다양한 에피소드 가운데에서 뼈대가 될 수 있는 것들을 정리하였고 암기보다는 이를 응용하여 쓸 수 있도록 하였다. 본 교재를 통해 학생들이 차근차근 학습하다 보면 어느덧 영어에 자신감이 붙고 영어 의사소통 능력이 향상될 것을 저자는 확신하는 바이다.

2017년 10월 30일

저자 조동인 씀.

목 차

Scene 1 How are you?

Talk 1-1.

Amy: Hi. How are you?

Kevin: I'm very good. How are you?

Amy: I'm so good, too.

Amy: It's a great day, isn't it?

Kevin: Yes it is. I really love sunny days.

Amy: Do you? I am happy you like sunny days like me.

Kevin: Oh, it's already ten to 9.
I'd better get going right now for the class. See you soon.

Amy: Bye, see you tomorrow.

Basic Expressions

a. How are you?
b. sunny days
c. I'd better get going.

Further Expressions

a. How have you been these days?
b. It couldn't be better.
c. It's already a quarter to ten.
d. See you in the near future.
e. I will keep my fingers crossed.

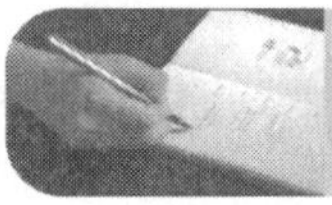

Review 1-1 A

1. **Choose the correct one for the blank.**
How ___ you?

a) are
b) is
c) has
d) have

2. **Choose the correct one for the blank.**
I'd better ______ going right now.

a) gets
b) getting
c) get
d) got

3. **Choose the one which is not appropriate for the blank.**
See you ________

a) tomorrow
b) next time
c) later
d) not

4. **Choose the one which is not appropriate for the blank.**
I really ______ sunny days.

a) like
b) love
c) hate
d) do

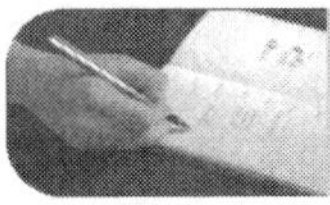

Review 1-1 B

1. **Choose the correct one for the blank.**
How _____ you been these days?

a) have
b) is
c) has
d) are

2. **Choose the correct one for the blank.**
The weather is so nice. and it couldn't be _____.

a) bat
b) bet
c) batter
d) better

3. **Choose the one which is not appropriate for the blank.**
It's already ________to ten.

a) a quarter
b) ten
c) five
d) second

4. **Choose the correct one for the blank.**
See you in the _____ future.

a) now
b) nearby
c) nest
d) near

Talk 1-2.

Kevin: Hi, Amy. How are you?
Amy: Fine, thanks. Kevin, this is Lisa.
Kevin: Hello, Lisa.
Lisa: How do you do?
Kevin: How do you do?
Lisa: Nice to meet you.
Kevin: Nice to meet you, too.
Kevin: Lisa, where are you from?
Lisa: I'm from New Zealand.
Kevin: Are you here on vacation?
Lisa: No. I'm here on business for a movie.
Kevin: What do you do?
Lisa: I'm a movie promoter.
Lisa: Kevin, what do you do?
Kevin: I'm a professional baseball player.

Basic Expressions

a. How do you do?
b. Nice to meet you.
c. What do you do?

Further Expressions

a. What do you do for a living?
b. What is your occupation?
c. May I ask what your occupation is?
d. You can't hide what your occupation is.
e. You can't hide what you do for a living.

Review 1-2 A

1. **Choose the correct one for the blank.**
How are you ______ ?

a) do
b) does
c) doing
d) done

2. **Choose the correct one for the blank.**
What is your ________?

a) occupy
b) occupant
c) occupied
d) occupation

3. **Choose the one which is not appropriate for the blank.**
A: What do you do?
B: __________________

a) I'm a movie star
b) My job is a teacher
c) I sleep late at night
d) I deliver goods to the clerks.

4. **Choose the one which is not appropriate for the blank.**
A: I'm ______ to meet you.

a) glad
b) happy
c) pleased
d) well

Review 1–2 B

1. **Choose the correct one for the blank.**
   What do you do for a _______?

   a) living
   b) live
   c) lives
   d) liver

2. **Choose the correct one for the blank.**
   I'm here _____ business.

   a) by
   b) on
   c) with
   d) over

3. **Choose the one which is not appropriate for the blank.**
   ______ I ask what your occupation is?

   a) May
   b) Can
   c) Do you mind if
   d) When do

4. **Choose the correct one for the blank.**
   You can't ______ what your occupation is

   a) hide
   b) hidden
   c) hides
   d) hiding

Scene 2 Where do you work?

Talk 2-1

Kevin: Where do you work?

Amy: I work for Korean Air.

Kevin: Oh, do you?

Kevin: What do you do for Korean Air?

Amy: I work as a stewardess.

Amy: Where do you work, Kavin?

Kevin: I work for the Korean government.

Amy: What do you mean by that?

Kevin: I am a public official.

Basic Expressions

a. Where do you work?
b. I work for the company.
c. I am a public official.

Further Expressions

a. I work as a flight attendant for Korean Air.
b. She is a member of cabin crew for Delta Airline.
c. What do you mean by that?
d. He is a high-level official in the diplomatic department.
e. My supervisor is in charge of the planning department.

Review 2-1 A

1. **Choose the correct one for the blank.**
Where do you ______ ?

a) work
b) works
c) working
d) worked

2. **Choose the correct one for the blank.**
I work ______ Johnson and Johnson Inc.

a) by
b) on
c) for
d) to

3. **Choose the correct one for the blank.**
Janet is a great flight ______ as I know.

a) attending
b) attend
c) attendant
d) attendants

4. **Choose the correct one for the blank.**
My supervisor is in _____of the planning department.

a) chance
b) charge
c) change
d) champion

Review 2-1 B

1. **Choose the correct one for the blank.**
She is a member of cabin _____ for Korean Air.

a) crew
b) cross
c) creek
d) cliff

2. **Choose the correct one for the blank.**
He is a high-level official ___ the diplomatic department.

a) by
b) on
c) in
d) to

3. **Choose the correct one for the blank.**
Jane's father is a public ______ for the government.

a) offer
b) office
c) official
d) offering

4. **Choose the correct one for the blank.**
What do you mean ______ ?

a) by those
b) by that
c) by us
d) by ours

Talk 2-2

Jenson: What are you doing now?

Kevin: I'm searching for a book about 3D printers.

Jenson: I'll buy a book on 3 D printers tomorrow.

Kevin: What did you say?

Jenson: I'll buy a book on 3 D printers.

Kevin: Really? Are you sure of the future of 3 D printers?

Jenson: Of course, would you give me some tips about 3 D printers?

Kevin: Ok, let me give you some.

Basic Expressions

a. I'm searching for a book.
b. I'll buy a book on 3 D printers.
c. Let me give you some.

Further Expressions

a. I'm in search of the books on Industrial Revolution.
b. Let me purchase a good tablet computer.
c. You need good tips on how to study English.
d. The expression of 3 D computer comes from 3 Dimensional printers.

Review 2-2 A

1. **Choose the correct one for the blank.**
I am________ for the business books for my homework.

a) searches
b) searcher
c) searching
d) search

2. **Choose the correct one for the blank.**
I'll buy a book _______3 D printers.

a) by
b) on
c) at
d) to

3. **Choose the correct one for the blank.**
Let me ______ you some good tips.

a) given
b) gives
c) give
d) giver

4. **Choose the correct one for the blank.**
Are you _____ of what you are talking to me?

a) assurance
b) sure
c) such
d) surfing

Review 2-2 B

1. **Choose the correct one for the blank.**
I'm in ______ of the books on Industrial Revolution.

a) search
b) searching
c) searches
d) searcher

2. **Choose the correct one for the blank.**
Let me _______ a good tablet computer.

a) purchases
b) purchasing
c) purchase
d) purchaser

3. **Choose the correct one for the blank.**
You need good tips ____ how to study English.

a) between
b) at
c) on
d) beneath

4. **Choose the correct one for the blank.**
3 D printers can produce three _________ objects.

a) dimension
b) dimensional
c) dimensions
d) dimensionals

Scene 3 Thank you for the invitation

Talk 3-1

Amy: Hi, Lisa. How have you been?

Lisa: Fine, thanks. Please make yourself comfortable.

Lisa: Lunch will be ready soon. Take a seat.

Amy: Oh, how kind you are. Thank you for your invitation to lunch.

Lisa: Please, help yourself.

Amy: Thanks a lot, your pasta is delicious.

Lisa: Would you like some more pasta?

Amy: Oh, yes, please. And may I have one more glass of soft drink?

Lisa: With my pleasure, here you are.

Amy: Wow, you must be an excellent cook.

Lisa: Thank you for your compliment.

Basic Expressions

a. Make yourself comfortable.
b. Help yourself
c. Thank you for your compliment.

Further Expressions

a. To have a party is a lot of fun.
b. The pasta is delicious and nothing to be desired.
c. The restaurant uses fresh ingredients for Pizza.
d. Jason likes to cook for himself.
e. Would you like another piece of apple pie?

Review 3-1 A

1. **Choose the correct one for the blank.**
Would you _______ some more food?

a) liked
b) likes
c) like
d) liking

2. **Choose the correct one for the blank.**
Please make yourself _________.

a) at house
b) at home
c) at desk
d) at night

3. **Choose the correct one for the blank.**
We prepared various kinds of food. ______ yourself.

a) Hell
b) Help
c) Hello
d) Hull

4. **Choose the correct one for the blank.**
Please, take a ______ for your lunch.

a) seats
b) sit down
c) sit
d) seat

Review 3-1 B

1. **Choose the correct one for the blank.**
To have a party _____ a lot of fun

a) been
b) is
c) does
d) be

2. **Choose the correct one for the blank.**
The restaurant uses _____ ingredients for Pizza.

a) fresh
b) freight
c) free
d) fraud

3. **Choose the correct one for the blank.**
Mr. Kim likes to _______ for himself.

a) cook
b) cooker
c) cooking
d) cooked

4. **Choose the correct one for the blank.**
Your food is great and nothing to be ________.

a) desirous
b) desires
c) desire
d) desired

Talk 3-2

Jenson: Thank you for the invitation to your housewarming.

Kevin: The pleasure is mine.

Kevin: Have you ever tried spicy Korean food?

Jenson: Yes, I love eating Tteokbokki. In other word, stir-fried rice cake in Korea, it's very hot.

Kevin: Well, you are right. To soothe the spicy taste some Koreans enjoy soup of fish cake together.

Jenson: You must be really busy preparing food for the party.

Kevin: My wife and I did our best to make homemade Tteokbokki.

Jenson: It's hot! But it is delicious.

Kevin: Thank you, please help yourself and also make yourself at home.

Basic Expressions

a. Thank you for the invitation to your housewarming.
b. You must be really busy preparing food for the party.
c. It's tasty.

Further Expressions

a. Homemade food is healthier than the restaurant food.
b. I work in a fast food restaurant.
c. She did her best to make delicious meal.
d. Hunger is the best source.
e. They put their heart into a meal for the baby.

Review 3-2 A

1. **Choose the correct one for the blank.**
You must ___ really busy preparing food for the party.

a) been
b) do
c) be
d) is

2. **Choose the correct one for the blank.**
Have you ever _____ spicy food?

a) tries
b) try
c) tried
d) trying

3. **Choose the correct one for the blank.**
Thank you for your ______ to lunch.

a) invite
b) invitation
c) invites
d) invitational

4. **Choose the one which is not appropriate for the blank.**
I really appreciate your ________ food for my birthday.

a) delicious
b) tasty
c) terrible
d) yummy

Review 3–2 B

1. **Choose the correct one for the blank.**
Homemade food is healthier _____ restaurant food.

a) then
b) that
c) than
d) this

2. **Choose the correct one for the blank.**
She did her best to _____ healthy food.

a) come
b) go
c) make
d) do

3. **Choose the correct one for the blank.**
They put their ____ into a meal for the baby.

a) heal
b) heart
c) hit
d) brain

4. **Choose the correct one for the blank.**
People say that _______ is the best source.

a) hunk
b) hungary
c) hungry
d) hunger

Scene 4 What can I do for you?

Talk 4-1

Clerk: What can I do for you?

Lisa: Good evening. I'm looking for a T-shirt.

Clerk: What color do you want?

Lisa: Red.

Clerk: And what kind of design do you want?

Lisa: I'm not sure.

Clerk: How about this shirt?

Lisa: Oh, it looks good. Can I try it on?

Clerk: Sure, you can.

Lisa: Thank you.

Lisa: How much does it cost?

Clerk: Forty thousand won.

Lisa: It sounds reasonable. Let me buy it.

Clerk: Thank you for your purchase.

Basic Expressions

a. What can I do for you?
b. How much does it cost?
c. It sounds reasonable.

Further Expressions

a. She works in the sales department.
b. They are having a clearance sale.
c. How may I help you?
e. Can I try it on?

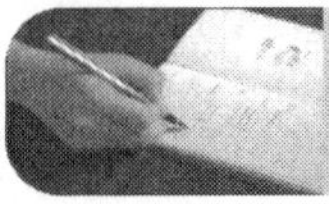

Review 4-1 A

1. **Choose the correct one for the blank.**
How ______ I help you?

a) been
b) done
c) may
d) am

2. **Choose the correct one for the blank.**
The T-shirt _______ great on you.

a) lookers
b) looking
c) looks
d) looker

3. **Choose the one which is not appropriate for the blank.**
My friend _______ a famous designer in the fashion industry.

a) is
b) are
c) has been
d) was

4. **Choose the correct one for the blank.**
She is looking _____ cheaper shirts to save living cost.

a) to
b) for
c) through
d) by

Review 4-1 B

1. **Choose the correct one for the blank.**
Can I try it _____ ?

a) over
b) on
c) to
d) before

2. **Choose the correct one for the blank.**
Mrs. Peterson works in the _____ department.

a) sell
b) sale
c) sales
d) sells

3. **Choose the correct one for the blank.**
How about _______ this T- shirt?

a) choosing
b) choice
c) choices
d) chosen

4. **Choose the correct one for the blank.**
The fashion outlet is having a _______ sale.

a) clarified
b) clearance
c) clarity
d) cliff

Talk 4-2

Lisa: Let me buy a back pack. How much is this?

Clerk: Good evening, it is normally one hundred dollars. But it is on sale for sixty dollars.

Lisa: It sounds good. Do you have other back packs on sale?

Clerk: Sure. We have a variety of new back packs on sale on the second floor.

Lisa: OK. Let me go upstairs.

Clerk: You can use the escalator over there.

Lisa: Which day is the last of the sale?

Clerk: Tomorrow is the last day. Thank you.

Basic Expressions

a. How much is this?
b. We have a variety of back packs.
c. Let me go upstairs.

Further Expressions

a. It will cost you five hundred dollars.
b. Sky is the limit.
c. Order whatever you want regardless of expense.
e. She wants to restrict expenditure on clothes.

Review 4–2 A

1. Choose the correct one for the blank.
_______ can I do for you?

a) What
b) Who
c) Where
d) Whose

2. Choose the correct one for the blank.

Do you have back packs _____ sale?

a) with
b) in
c) on
d) over

3. Choose the correct one for the blank.
The shop has a _______ of goods on sports.

a) various
b) vary
c) variety
d) varying

4. Choose the correct one for the blank.
_______ me go upstairs for other goods.

a) Let's
b) Let us
c) Let
d) Lets

Review 4-2 B

1. **Choose the correct one for the blank.**
A: How much is this back pack?
B: It will cost ______ eighty thousand one.

a) you
b) yours
c) you're
d) your

2. **Choose the correct one for the blank.**
She wants to buy her new mobile phone ______ of expense.

a) regarding
b) regard
c) regardless
d) regards

3. **Choose the correct one for the blank.**
The boss of the company restricts ______ on paper consumption.

a) express
b) extra
c) expenditure
d) exclusive

4. **Choose the correct one for the blank.**
Save ______ money for your future.

a) extreme
b) active
c) extra
d) acute

Scene 5 What would you like to order?

Talk 5-1

Server: Can I take your order, sir?
Jenson: What is the popular dish at this restaurant?
Server: The T-bone steak is the most popular menu.
Jenson: And then, let me have a T-bone steak.
Server: How would you like your steak, sir?
Jenson: Rare, please.
Server: Do you need anything to drink?
Jenson: A glass of orange juice with ice, please.
Server: Let me serve you right away with what you have ordered.
Jenson: Thank you.

Basic Expressions

a. Can I take your order?
b. How would you like your steak?
c. A glass of orange juice, please.

Further Expressions

a. In order to lose weight she is on a diet.
b. Her religion demands dietary control.
c. Many dieters know they should not eat food late at night.
d. He eats less and works out on a regular basis.

Review 5-1 A

1. **Choose the correct one for the blank.**
Do you mind if I _____ your order?

a) taking
b) taken
c) take
d) takes

2. **Choose the correct one for the blank.**
How would you ______ your steak?

a) likes
b) like
c) liking
d) liked

3. **Choose the one which is not appropriate for the blank.**
A: Do you need anything to drink?
B: ________________

a) A glass of wine, please
b) A can of seven-up, please
c) A bottle of mineral water, please
d) A piece of blanket, please

4. **Choose the correct one for the blank.**
In _____ to lose weight, she works out everyday.

a) have
b) order
c) take
d) go

Review 5–1 B

1. **Choose the correct one for the blank.**
She is ____ a diet, since she wants to look slim.

a) to
b) over
c) on
d) between

2. **Choose the correct one for the blank.**
Her religion ________ dietary control.

a) demand
b) demands
c) demanding
d) to demand

3. **Choose the correct one for the blank.**
You should not eat food ______ at night if you are on a diet.

a) little
b) least
c) last
d) late

4. **Choose the correct one for the blank.**
I eat less and work out on a regular ______.

a) base
b) bat
c) best
d) basis

Talk 5–2

Server: What would you like to order, sir?

Jenson: Let me have a slice of potato pizza and a can of coke.

Jenson: What would you like to have, Amy?

Amy: Let me take a look at the menu.

Server: Cheese pizza is the specialty at our restaurant.

Amy: Why your cheese pizza is special?

Server: We import fresh and gourmet cheese from the local farms in France directly.

Amy: It sounds good. Let me try cheese pizza.

Server: Will you have a drink?

Amy: Yes, a glass of sprite, but without ice.

Server: I see, ma'am. Let me serve you soon with your food.

Amy: Thank you for your kindness.

Basic Expressions

a. What would you like to have?
b. Let me take a look at the menu.
c. Let me serve you soon.

Further Expressions

a. She enjoys gourmet food at the restaurant.

b. They ate shark's fin soup, a delicacy in China.

c. Food poisoning is a serious disease during the summer season.

d. The recipe of the restaurant uses innovative ingredients.

Review 5-2 A

1. **Choose the correct one for the blank.**
Can I take your _____ ?

a) ordering
b) ordered
c) order
d) to order

2. **Choose the correct one for the blank.**
Cheese pizza is the ________ at this restaurant.

a) special
b) specialty
c) specialize
d) specialized

3. **Choose the one which is not appropriate for the blank.**
A: What would you like to order?
B: _______________

a) A glass of wine, please
b) A slice of pizza
c) Rare, please
d) Firstly, let me take a look at the menu.

4. **Choose the one which is not appropriate for the blank.**
What would you like to ______?

a) have
b) order
c) take
d) go

Review 5–2 B

1. **Choose the correct one for the blank.**
Let me have a ______ of potato pizza.

a) slow
b) sleep
c) slice
d) slip

2. **Choose the correct one for the blank.**
She enjoys the _______ food at the restaurant.

a) gone
b) gourmet
c) ghost
d) go

3. **Choose the correct one for the blank.**
They ate shark’ s fin soup, a ______ in China.

a) deal
b) deliberate
c) delicacy
d) delight

4. **Choose the correct one for the blank.**
Food _____ is a serious disease during the summer season.

a) pottery
b) poem
c) post
d) poisoning

Scene 6 At the post office

Talk 6-1

Jenson: Good morning, I'd like to send this parcel by registered post.

Clerk: You have two options, by air or by sea.

Jenson: By air please, and also by special delivery.

Clerk: Is there anything valuable inside the parcel?

Jenson: Nothing valuable

Clerk: Do you have any dangerous or illegal items in it?

Jenson: Don't worry about it. It is just a book.

Clerk: Okay, it will be fifty five dollars.

Jenson: Can I use my credit card here?

Clerk: No problem, sir.

Basic Expressions

a. Send a parcel by registered mail.
b. by air or by sea
c. by special delivery

Further Expressions

a. How far is the nearest post office from here?
b. Enter your zip code or postal code for the address.
c. Any recipient should be at home at time of delivery.
d. How much will it cost to send this by overnight mail?

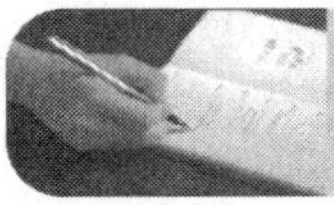

Review 6-1 A

1. **Choose the correct one for the blank.**
Let me ______ this letter by special mail?

a) sending
b) sender
c) send
d) sends

2. **Choose the correct one for the blank.**
The postage of air mail is more ______ than that of regular mail.

a) extending
b) extend
c) expensive
d) expansion

3. **Choose the one which is not appropriate for the blank.**
Thank you for your ________.

a) advice
b) tips
c) kind
d) purchase

4. **Choose the correct one for the blank.**
_________ requires to be adhered on the envelope.

a) Post
b) Postage
c) Portal
d) Pork

Review 6–1 B

1. **Choose the correct one for the blank.**
How ____ is the nearest post office from here?

a) front
b) free
c) far
d) feeling

2. **Choose the correct one for the blank.**
Enter your zip code or ______ code for the address.

a) poster
b) posting
c) postal
d) position

3. **Choose the correct one for the blank.**
Any recipient should be ___ home at time of delivery.

a) to
b) with
c) at
d) between

4. **Choose the correct one for the blank.**
How much will it cost to send this by_______ mail?

a) night
b) over
c) overnight
d) day

Talk 6-2

Clerk: Next customer, please.

Amy: Good afternoon, let me send this letter by air.

Clerk: By registered mail or ordinary mail?

Amy: By ordinary mail, please.

Clerk: You should pay 24 dollars for it.

Amy: Okay, let me see. I am searching for my wallet.

Clerk: Both cash and credit card will do. Will you pay by cash or credit card?

Amy: I don't carry any credit cards. Here is three ten-dollar bills.

Clerk: Thank you. Take the postage and your change.

Amy: Oh, thank you. I appreciate your kindness.

Basic Expressions

a. By ordinary mail
b. Will you pay by cash or credit card?
c. Thank you for your kindness.

Further Expressions

a. A post office distinguishes between ordinary mail and express mail
b. The new mailing system of the country is second to none in the world
c. The email system has been disabled due to technical errors
d. You can send him an email

Review 6-2 A

1. **Choose the correct one for the blank.**
A post office deals ______ many kinds of mails.

a) to
b) at
c) with
d) out

2. **Choose the correct one for the blank.**
Will you pay ______cash or credit card?

a) for
b) by
c) before
d) after

3. **Choose the correct one for the blank.**
A post office distinguishes ______ ordinary mail and express mail.

a) to
b) with
c) between
d) before

4. **Choose the correct one for the blank.**
The new mailing system of the country is ______ to none.

a) first
b) set
c) second
d) center

Review 6–2 B

1. **Choose the correct one for the blank.**
The email system has been disabled _____ technical errors.

a) thanks
b) owe
c) due to
d) due

2. **Choose the correct one for the blank.**
You can _____ me an email if it is necessary.

a) sends
b) send
c) sending
d) sender

3. **Choose the correct one for the blank.**
Email comes from the expression of _______ mail.

a) electrician
b) electricity
c) electronic
d) electric

4. **Choose the correct one for the blank.**
If you need to send a parcel, _______ it is essential.

a) wait
b) weight
c) weighing
d) waiter

Scene 7 Hold on a minute

Talk 7-1

Jenson: Hello.

Amy: Hello, is Thompson there?

Jenson: Yes, he is. Who's calling, please?

Amy: This is Amy speaking.

Jenson: Hi, Amy. Thompson, it's for you. It's Amy. Hold on a minute, please.

Thompson: Hi, Amy. How was the dinner yesterday?

Amy: It was fantastic. I could have a good time due to your kindness.

Thompson: I am happy to hear that. Shall we go out tonight, too?

Amy: Okay. See you after work.

Basic Expressions

a. Who is calling, please?
b. It was fantastic.
c. I am happy to hear that.

Further Expressions

a. I'd like to place a collect call to New York.
b. Please ring me back in an hour.
c. Jenson calls you on the telephone.
d. Let's call it a day!

Review 7-1 A

1. **Choose the correct one for the blank.**
Who is ______ please?

a) calling
b) call
c) calls
d) called

2. **Choose the correct one for the blank.**
______ is Amy speaking.

a) This
b) That
c) These
d) Those

3. **Choose the correct one for the blank.**
Hi, Amy, ______ was the dinner, yesterday?

a) how
b) which
c) who
d) whose

4. **Choose the one which is not appropriate for the blank.**
The dinner was ____________.

a) fantastic
b) great
c) nothing to be desired
d) nobody

Review 7–1 B

1. **Choose the correct one for the blank.**
I'd like to place a ______ call to Japan.

a) calling
b) caller
c) collection
d) collect

2. **Choose the correct one for the blank.**
Please ______ me back when you are free.

a) ring
b) calls
c) ringing
d) calling

3. **Choose the correct one for the blank.**
Dr. Hamilton calls you _____ the telephone.

a) on
b) to
c) with
d) before

4. **Choose the correct one for the blank.**
We have finished today's work. Let's call it a _____!

a) data
b) dance
c) date
d) day

Talk 7-2

Amy: Hello?

Jenson: Good afternoon. Can I speak to Thompson at the department of accounting?

Amy: Hold on a moment please. Let me see whether he is in or not.

Amy: Hello? I am sorry to say that he is not in his room.

Jenson: Well, then can I leave a message for him?

Amy: Of course. Can you tell me who is calling?

Jenson: Jenson is speaking. Please tell him to call me back. He knows my phone number.

Amy: OK. Let me definitely carry the message.

Basic Expressions

a. Hold on a moment.
b. Can I leave a message for him?
c. Please tell him to call me back.

Further Expressions

a. Please hold on, I'll connect you with him.
b. She saved her father with the help of a 911 operator.
c. When you want to disconnect, hang up the phone.
d. If you need anything, pick up the phone and call me.
e. Let me transfer you to my boss.

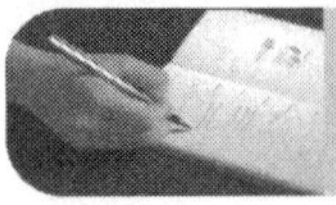

Review 7–2 A

1. **Choose the correct one for the blank.**
Please, _____ on a moment.

a) hold
b) holds
c) holding
d) holder

2. **Choose the correct one for the blank.**
Let me see ______ he is in or not.

a) which
b) whether
c) when
d) who

3. **Choose the correct one for the blank.**
Can I leave a _______ for him.

a) mart
b) moment
c) message
d) money

4. **Choose the correct one for the blank.**
Please, ____ him to call me back later.

a) told
b) telling
c) tell
d) teller

Review 7-2 B

1. **Choose the correct one for the blank.**
I'll _______ you with him within a minute.

a) connects
b) connection
c) connecting
d) connect

2. **Choose the correct one for the blank.**
She saved her pet with the help of a 911 _____.

a) operate
b) operator
c) operates
d) operated

3. **Choose the correct one for the blank.**
When you want to _______, hang up the phone.

a) disconnecter
b) disconnected
c) disconnects
d) disconnect

4. **Choose the correct one for the blank.**
If you need anything, _____ up the phone and call me.

a) kick
b) dick
c) pick
d) tick

Scene 8 Transportation

Talk 8-1

Jenson: How do you get to work?

Amy: I take the subway everyday, but sometimes by bus. How about you?

Jenson: By bus. But it is very difficult for me to use crowded buses during the rush hours.

Amy: What time do you catch the bus?

Jenson: Almost at 8:00

Amy: How long does it take you to get to work by bus?

Jenson: About half an hour.

Amy: Then, you will be happy with the short distance.
It takes me one hour and a half to get to work. I envy you.

Basic Expressions

a. How do you get to work?
b. I take subway everyday.
c. How long does it take?

Further Expressions

a. Many people travel to work either by bus or by subway.
b. She lives in a suburb and commutes to the city every day.
c. The commuter bus is always crowded.
d. I left my house early but I missed a bus.

Review 8-1 A

1. **Choose the correct one for the blank.**
______ do you get to work?

a) Whose
b) Which
c) How
d) What

2. **Choose the correct one for the blank.**
______ do you catch the bus?

a) What time
b) What
c) Who
d) Whose

3. **Choose the one which is not appropriate for the blank.**
I go to work by ______.

a) bus
b) subway
c) a taxi
d) train

4. **Choose the correct one for the blank.**
______ does it take to get to work?

a) What
b) How
c) How long
d) Whose

Review 8–1 B

1. **Choose the correct one for the blank.**
Many people _______ to work either by bus or by subway.

a) traveling
b) traveler
c) travel
d) travels

2. **Choose the correct one for the blank.**
They live in a suburb and _______ to the office day after day.

a) commutes
b) commuters
c) commute
d) commuting

3. **Choose the one which is not appropriate for the blank.**
The commuter bus is always _______.

a) busy
b) crowded
c) late
d) starter

4. **Choose the correct one for the blank.**
I left my house _______ but I missed a bus.

a) early
b) now
c) new
d) late

Talk 8–2

Amy: Excuse me, can you tell me where I can buy a ticket?

Amy: Go straight down, and then turn right at the corner. You'll see a ticket window,

Amy: Thank you, it's very kind of you.

Amy: The pleasure is mine.

Amy: Good afternoon. I'd like to buy a ticket to Los Angeles.

Ticket Officer: What do you want? one way or round trip?

Amy: Round trip, please. How much is it?

Ticket Officer: That will be 80 dollars.

Basic Expressions

a. The pleasure is mine.
b. I'd like to buy a ticket to Los Angeles.
c. One way or round trip?

Further Expressions

a. How long have you been behind the wheel?
b. We have run out of gas along the way.
c. I am looking for a gas station.
d. She was embarrassed because of a traffic jam.
e. I hate traffic congestion early in the morning.

Review 8-2 A

1. Choose the correct one for the blank.
It is very ______ of you, thank you.

a) kind
b) kindness
c) happy
d) happiness

2. Choose the correct one for the blank.
I'd like to ______ a ticket to Busan.

a) buy
b) bought
c) by
d) be

3. Choose the one which is not appropriate for the blank.
A: Thank you for your help.
B: ____________________

a) The pleasure is mine
b) You're welcome
c) It is my pleasure
d) Think twice.

4. Choose the correct one for the blank.
What do you want? one way or ______ trip?

a) rope
b) roll
c) round
d) rotary

Review 8-2 B

1. **Choose the correct one for the blank.**
How long have you been ______ the wheel?

a) between
b) behind
c) within
d) of

2. **Choose the correct one for the blank.**
We have run out of _____ along the way.

a) gas
b) gases
c) gap
d) gasket

3. **Choose the one which is not appropriate for the blank.**
She was _______ because of a traffic jam.

a) embarrassed
b) tired
c) mad
d) happiness

4. **Choose the correct one for the blank.**
We hate _______ congestion early in the morning.

a) tree
b) trout
c) trouble
d) traffic

Scene 9 What is your favorite season?

Talk 9-1

Jenson: Amy, what is your favorite season?

Amy: Summer is my favorite.

Jenson: Do you have any special reason?

Amy: That's because I love surfing at the beach.

Jenson: Kate, what about you?

Kate: I like spring best. Do you know why?

Jenson: I want to know the reason.

Kate: Because I love strolling down the path of cherry blossoms.

Kate: Jenson, which season do you like?

Jenson: I like autumn, since I love crisp air during the season.

Basic Expressions

a. I love surfing at the beach.
b. What is your favorite season?
c. Which season do you like?

Further Expressions

a. Some people look forward to meeting the seasonal change.
b. They are out of season this time of the year.
c. The scenery of Mt. Sorak varies from season to season.
d. The tropical night phenomenon has increased these days.

Review 9-1 A

1. **Choose the correct one for the blank.**
What is your _____ season?

a) favor
b) favorite
c) fates
d) fate

2. **Choose the correct one for the blank.**
I love ______ down the path of cherry blossoms.

a) stroller
b) strolls
c) stroll
d) strolling

3. **Choose the one which is not appropriate for the blank.**
I ________ crisp air during the season.

a) like
b) love
c) enjoy
d) fall

4. **Choose the correct one for the blank.**
I wan to know the ______ of your being late everyday.

a) repetition
b) reasonable
c) reason
d) reaction

Review 9-1 B

1. **Choose the correct one for the blank.**
Some people look forward to ______ the seasonal change.

a) have been met
b) meeting
c) met
d) meets

2. **Choose the correct one for the blank.**
Watermelon is out of ______ this time of year.

a) seasonings
b) seasoning
c) seasonal
d) season

3. **Choose the one which is not appropriate for the blank.**
I ______ autumn because of my hobby.

a) like
b) love
c) enjoy
d) fall

4. **Choose the correct one for the blank.**
The scenery of the country varies ______ season to season.

a) behind
b) for
c) from
d) at

Talk 9-2

Amy: Which season do you like best, Jenson?

Jenson: I love autumn. Autumn is the best season to read books.

Amy: Really? do you like to read books?

Jenson: Yes, reading is my favorite hobby. The weather of autumn is good for reading.

Amy: Reading should be a part of your life, not hobby.

Jenson: You're definitely right. I try to read a book every day.

Amy: You have a good habit of reading. Reading can enrich your life.

Jenson: That's true. Reading can change our life.

Basic Expressions

a. Reading is my favorite hobby.
b. The weather of autumn is good for reading.
c. You have a good habit.

Further Expressions

a. During autumn many trees change their color.
b. In Korea winter is the great season to enjoy skiing.
c. Some animals are nocturnal because they are active at night.
d. They have traveled night and day for a week

Review 9-2 A

1. **Choose the correct one for the blank.**
Which season do you like _____?

a) bat
b) bets
c) bests
d) best

2. **Choose the correct one for the blank.**
Autumn is the best season to ______ books.

a) read
b) reads
c) reader
d) readers

3. **Choose the one which is not appropriate for the blank.**
Reading can enrich __________.

a) we
b) us
c) your life
d) yourself

4. **Choose the correct one for the blank.**
You have a good ______ of reading.

a) herb
b) habitual
c) habitat
d) habit

Review 9–2 B

1. **Choose the correct one for the blank.**
_______ summer I can enjoy swimming at the beach.

a) Which
b) Between
c) Because
d) During

2. **Choose the correct one for the blank.**
In Korea spring is the best season to _____ cherry blossom festival.

a) enjoy
b) enjoyable
c) enjoys
d) enjoyed

3. **Choose the one which is not appropriate for the blank.**
Some animals are nocturnal, _______ they are active at night.

a) on account of
b) because
c) as
d) since

4. **Choose the correct one for the blank.**
They have traveled night and ______ for a week.

a) time
b) season
c) date
d) day

Scene 10 Directions

Talk 10-1

Jenson: Excuse me. I'm looking for a city library. Is there a library in this town?

Thompson: Of course.

Jenson: Can you tell me the way to the place?

Thompson: No problem. Go down one block from here, and then turn to the left. You'll find it easily.

Jenson: Is it far from here?

Thompson: No, it is very near from here. It's only a ten- minute walk to the library.

Jenson: Thank you. It's very kind of you.

Thompson: It is my pleasure.

Basic Expressions

a. I'm looking for a city library.
b. Can you tell me the way to the place?
c. It's only a ten- minute walk

Further Expressions

a. I went sightseeing around the Grand Canyon one year ago.
b. Namdaemun is a must for foreign tourists.
c. The cafeteria is on the second floor of the orange building.
d. The college is located in front of a small hill.

Review 10-1 A

1. **Choose the correct one for the blank.**
Can you tell me the _____ to City Hall?

a) party
b) moment
c) way
d) song

2. **Choose the correct one for the blank.**
Is it far _____ here?

a) by
b) from
c) to
d) at

3. **Choose the one which is not appropriate for the blank.**
I am _______ a city library.

a) looking for
b) searching for
c) seeking
d) finding for

4. **Choose the correct one for the blank.**
It's only a ten- minute _____ to the library.

a) walked
b) walks
c) walk
d) walker

Review 10-1 B

1. **Choose the correct one for the blank.**
She ______ to Switzerland one year ago.

a) gone
b) goes
c) went
d) go

2. **Choose the correct one for the blank.**

His office is _____ the second floor of this building.

a) by
b) off
c) on
d) at

3. **Choose the one which is not appropriate for the blank.**
Mt. Halla is a ________ for foreign tourists.

a) good place
b) must
c) tourist spot
d) can

4. **Choose the correct one for the blank.**
The college is located _____ front of a small hill.

a) from
b) at
c) in
d) with

Talk 10-2

Jenson: Is this the right way to the Seoul station?

Thompson: Yes, it is.

Jenson: Can I go there by bus?

Thompson: Yes, you can. It will take 20 minutes from here to the place by bus.

Jenson: What number of the bus should I take?

Thompson: You should take the bus of the blue line. The bus number is 122.

Jenson: Thank you very much.

Thompson: No, problem. My pleasure.

Basic Expressions

a. Is this the right way to the Seoul station?
b. Can I go there by bus?
c. It will take 20 minutes by bus.

Further Expressions

a. The bus stop is within three minutes' walk from my house.
b. Is there a train station nearby?
c. Do not make a U-turn in the middle of the road without signs.
d. Seoul is well equipped with the regular bus service.

Review 10-2 A

1. Choose the correct one for the blank.
Is this the ____ to Itaewon?

a) man
b) shop
c) way
d) soap

2. Choose the correct one for the blank.
Can I go there ___ train?

a) over
b) beyond
c) with
d) by

3. Choose the one which is not appropriate for the blank.
You should take the bus of ________.

a) blue line
b) red line
c) No. 122.
d) rules

4. Choose the correct one for the blank.
What kind of bus should I _______ ?

a) taken
b) takes
c) take
d) taking

Review 10-2 B

1. **Choose the correct one for the blank.**
The bus terminal is _____ five minutes' walk from my house.

a) what
b) which
c) with
d) within

2. **Choose the correct one for the blank.**
Is there a bus station _______?

a) most
b) mostly
c) nearly
d) nearby

3. **Choose the one which is not appropriate for the blank.**
Seoul is ________ the regular bus service.

a) well equipped with
b) famous for
c) a good city for us to use
d) looked for

4. **Choose the correct one for the blank.**
Do not ______ a U-turn in the middle of the road without signs.

a) make
b) making
c) take
d) taking

Scene 11 Reservation

Talk 11-1

Staff: Good afternoon, what can I do for you?

Thompson: Good afternoon. Isn't Korean Air reservation department? I'd like to make an airline ticket reservation.

Staff: Yes, this is reservation department, sir. Where are you going?

Thompson: To Los Angeles

Staff: When are you leaving?

Thompson: Upcoming Saturday

Staff: What time are you going to leave?

Thompson: At 9:30 in the morning.

Staff: Good. your airline ticket has been booked now.

Thompson: I appreciate your kindness and help.

Staff: You're welcome. Have a nice day.

Basic Expressions

a. I'd like to make an airline reservation.
b. When are you leaving?
c. Your airline ticket has been booked.

Further Expressions

a. The arrival of the flight has been delayed due to bad weather.
b. Baggage is being claimed at the airline terminal.
c. Where can I buy a cheap airline ticket on the internet?
d. Where is the final destination of your trip?

Review 11-1 A

1. **Choose the correct one for the blank.**
______ time are you going to leave?

a) What
b) When
c) Whose
d) Who

2. **Choose the correct one for the blank.**
I ________ your kindness and help.

a) appreciate
b) appreciates
c) appreciating
d) appreciation

3. **Choose the one which is not appropriate for the blank.**
When are you ______ ?

a) leaving
b) going
c) arriving
d) seeing

4. **Choose the correct one for the blank.**
Your airline ticket has been ______ now.

a) booking
b) books
c) book
d) booked

Review 11-1 B

1. **Choose the correct one for the blank.**
The arrival of the flight has been ______ due to bad weather.

a) delayed
b) driven
c) taken
d) brought

2. **Choose the correct one for the blank.**
How many pieces of ________ are you carrying?

a) baggage
b) baggages
c) luggages
d) furnitures

3. **Choose the one which is not appropriate for the blank.**
Where can I _____ a cheap airline ticket on the internet?

a) buy
b) purchase
c) get
d) attend

4. **Choose the correct one for the blank.**
Where is the final _________ of your trip?

a) deletion
b) delight
c) destiny
d) destination

Talk 11-2

Staff: Good morning, Korean Air. How may I help you?

Amy: Good morning, let me reserve a flight ticket to New Mexico from Incheon Airport.

Staff: When is your departure date?

Amy: Next Thursday, March 22nd. Can I leave as early as possible on that day?

Staff: You can leave at 8:30 at the earliest in the morning,

Amy: Not bad. let me take it.

Staff: Okay. You have a reservation to New Mexico from Incheon on Thursday, March 22nd at 8;30. Is it one way or round trip?

Amy: One way, please

Staff: Okay, your one way ticket has been reserved. Please check in at least one and half an hour before departure time. Thank you.

Basic Expressions

a. How may I help you?
b. You can leave at 8:30 in the morning.
c. One way or round trip?

Further Expressions

a. The airplane No. KE 122 is taking off from Incheon airport.
b. Do you have anything to declare?
c. The airplane is landing on the runway.
d. You need to fill out the customs declaration form.

Review 11–2 A

1. **Choose the correct one for the blank.**
How _____ I help you?

a) does
b) are
c) may
d) dare

2. **Choose the correct one for the blank.**
You can leave at 8:30 at the _______ in the morning.

a) early
b) earliest
c) yearly
d) year

3. **Choose the one which is not appropriate for the blank.**
Not bad. let me ______ it.

a) choose
b) have
c) walk
d) take

4. **Choose the correct one for the blank.**
You have a_________ of flight ticket to New Mexico.

a) reserving
b) reserves
c) reservation
d) reserve

Review 11-2 B

1. **Choose the correct one for the blank.**
The airplane is ______ off from Incheon airport.

a) takes
b) take
c) taking
d) taken

2. **Choose the correct one for the blank.**
Do you have anything to ________?

a) declares
b) declare
c) declaring
d) declaration

3. **Choose the one which is not appropriate for the blank.**
The airplane ___________ Gimpo airport.

a) is landing on
b) takes off from
c) arrives at
d) is going

4. **Choose the correct one for the blank.**
You need to _____ out the customs declaration form.

a) pull
b) pill
c) fill
d) full

Scene 12 Disease

Talk 12-1

Jenson: Hi, Amy. It's time for lunch. What do you want to have for lunch?

Amy: Thank you for your offer, but I am suffering from diarrhea.

Jenson: That's too bad. When were you feeling bad ?

Amy: Since last night I've been so sick and even vomitting.

Jenson: And then, you'd better leave work early and see a doctor.

Amy: You're right. Thank you for your consideration.

Jenson: Don't mention it. Let me give you a ride to a hospital if you need.

Amy: How sweet you are. You look like an angel.

Basic Expressions

a. What do you want to have for lunch?
b. I am suffering from diarrhea.
c. Let me give you a ride to a hospital.

Further Expressions

a. Jenson called in sick early in the morning.
b. Does your insurance policy cover surgery?
c. Antibiotics can help you recover from a number of illnesses.
d. He caught a cold last night.
e. She got infected with a severe influenza.

Review 12-1 A

1. **Choose the correct one for the blank.**
What do you want to have _____ lunch?

a) behind
b) in
c) for
d) to

2. **Choose the correct one for the blank.**
I am ________ from diarrhea.

a) surf
b) surfing
c) suffer
d) suffering

3. **Choose the one which is not appropriate for the blank.**
I was so ______ and even vomitting.

a) sick
b) tired
c) exhausted
d) happy

4. **Choose the correct one for the blank.**
Let me give you a _____ to a hospital.

a) walk
b) walks
c) ride
d) rides

Review 12-1 B

1. **Choose the correct one for the blank.**
Jenson called in _____ early in the morning.

a) illness
b) ill
c) sick
d) sickness

2. **Choose the correct one for the blank.**
My insurance policy _______ even surgery.

a) have covered
b) cover
c) covering
d) covers

3. **Choose the one which is not appropriate for the blank.**
______ can help you recover from a number of illnesses.

a) Some drug
b) Some medicine
c) Antibiotics
d) Ailment

4. **Choose the correct one for the blank.**
He _______ a severe cold last night.

a) caught
b) made
c) exhausted
d) took

Talk 12-2

Jenson: Amy, have you been feeling bad until now?

Amy: Yes, I have been suffering from backache, and arthritis of my right arm.

Jenson: Did you take any pills to cure your symptoms?

Amy: I'd love to. But I couldn't see a doctor due to my busy schedule.

Jenson: Let me take over your work, and you can leave early.

Amy: Thank you for your kindness, but I am afraid of my stubborn boss.

Jenson: Don't worry about it. Our boss is out of town now for our clients.
But he'll understand it.

Amy: All right, let's make a reservation call to the hospital first.

Jenson: It sounds like a good idea.

Basic Expressions

a. Take a pill to cure your symptoms.
b. Let me take it over.
c. He is out of town now.

Further Expressions

a. You look very tired, you'd better take a rest
b. She is always careful of taking medicine
c. The regular medical checkup is necessary for your health
d. Dr. Jenson is a skilled and much experienced physician

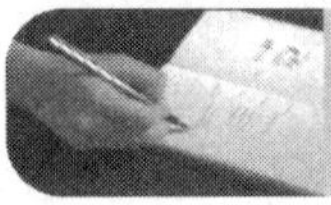

Review 12–2 A

1. **Choose the correct one for the blank.**
Did you _____ any pills to cure your symptoms?

a) takes
b) take
c) taken
d) took

2. **Choose the correct one for the blank.**
Let me take ______ your work.

a) by
b) beyond
c) with
d) over

3. **Choose the one which is not appropriate for the blank.**
Don't ______________ it.

a) worry about
b) mention
c) touch
d) look

4. **Choose the correct one for the blank.**
I am afraid ___ my supervisor when he is angry.

a) after
b) with
c) of
d) on

Review 12-2 B

1. **Choose the correct one for the blank.**
She looks very tired, and she'd better ______ a rest.

a) takes
b) take
c) taken
d) took

2. **Choose the correct one for the blank.**
She is always careful ______ taking medicine.

a) by
b) off
c) with
d) of

3. **Choose the one which is not appropriate for the blank.**
Dr. Cruz is a/an ___________ physician.

a) skilled
b) experienced
c) good
d) newly

4. **Choose the correct one for the blank.**
The regular______ checkup is necessary for your health.

a) medicinal
b) medic
c) medical
d) medicine

Scene 13 Travel

Talk 13-1

Jenson: I'm going to travel Canada this weekend. Have you ever traveled Canada?

Amy: No, how many countries have you visited?

Jenson: Two countries until now. I've traveled U.S.A and New Zealand.

Amy: I envy you. Will you travel more countries in the near future?

Jenson: Absolutely. I want to travel as many countries as possible.

Amy: Wow, you enjoy your life well.

Jenson: I am just trying to live my life as I want to.

Amy: You are the real master of your life. Have a good trip to Canada during your leave.

Basic Expressions

a. Have you ever traveled Canada?
b. Can you tell me the way to the place?
c. Have a good trip to Canada during your leave.

Further Expressions

a. She wants to travel all over the world.
b. A traveler stopped to have a rest under a tree.
c. He left for a business trip two days ago.
d. I was on an ocean voyage when you called me.

Review 13-1 A

1. **Choose the correct one for the blank.**
Have you ________ traveled Canada?

a) event
b) eve
c) every
d) ever

2. **Choose the correct one for the blank.**
I've ________ Korea and China in my life.

a) travel
b) traveled
c) travels
d) travelling

3. **Choose the one which is not appropriate for the blank.**
I am just trying to _____ my life well.

a) enjoy
b) look
c) live
d) lead

4. **Choose the correct one for the blank.**
Have a good ______ to Canada during your leave.

a) trip
b) tripping
c) traveler
d) trouble

Review 13-1 B

1. **Choose the correct one for the blank.**
Ms. McCarthy wants to travel all ______ the world.

a) on
b) at
c) to
d) over

2. **Choose the correct one for the blank.**
A tourist has stopped to ______ a rest under a tree.

a) have
b) do
c) travel
d) move

3. **Choose the correct one for the blank.**
He ______ for a business trip two days ago.

a) took
b) left
c) live
d) led

4. **Choose the correct one for the blank.**
I was on a ocean ______ when you called me.

a) voyage
b) tripping
c) buoy
d) poll

Talk 13-2

Jenson: Have you ever been to Tokyo?

Thompson: Yes, I've been there twice.

Jenson: How was the trip to Tokyo?

Thompson: It was fantastic. I especially enjoyed sushi and raw fish.

Jenson: Would you recommend a tourist spot in Tokyo?
I go to Tokyo for my leave with my family.

Thompson: Of course. I strongly recommend Hakone for your leave.

Jenson: Why do you recommend Hakone?

Thompson: Hakone is famous for hot spring and a serene forest.
It is not that far from the heart of Tokyo.

Jenson: It sounds great. Thank you for your recommendation.

Thompson: Your welcome. Hopefully you enjoy your trip to Tokyo,

Basic Expressions

a. Have you ever been to Tokyo?
b. Would you recommend a tourist spot in Korea?
c. Hopefully you enjoy your trip to Tokyo.

Further Expressions

a. The renovated amusement park has become a tourist attraction.
b. I went to a travel agency to buy a cheap air ticket.
c. A travel agent booked her hotel reservation.
d. The concierge can help you with your needs during your stay.

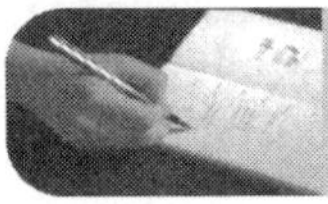

Review 13–2 A

1. **Choose the correct one for the blank.**
Have you ever _______ to Tokyo?

a) be
b) is
c) been
d) are

2. **Choose the correct one for the blank.**
Would you _______ a tourist spot in Tokyo?

a) recommend
b) recommending
c) recommendable
d) recommends

3. **Choose the one which is not appropriate for the blank.**
A travel ______ booked our hotel reservation.

a) agent
b) agency
c) conductor
d) tutor

4. **Choose the correct one for the blank.**
The concierge can help you ____ your needs during your stay.

a) at
b) between
c) to
d) with

Review 13-2 B

1. **Choose the correct one for the blank.**
The renovated amusement park has become a tourist ______.

a) attractive
b) attracting
c) attraction
d) attracts

2. **Choose the correct one for the blank.**
She went to a travel _______ to buy a cheap air ticket.

a) agenda
b) aging
c) age
d) agency

3. **Choose the one which is not appropriate for the blank.**
Hakone ______ famous for hot spring and a serene forest.

a) has been
b) was
c) is
d) does

4. **Choose the correct one for the blank.**
Hopefully you ________ your trip to Tokyo.

a) enjoys
b) enjoying
c) enjoy
d) enjoyable

Scene 14 Job Interview

Talk 14-1

Jenson: Good morning. I came here for my job interview.

Secretary: Wait a moment, please. Can you tell me your name?

Jenson: I'm Jenson.

Secretary: What's your sur name?

Jenson: Cruz

Secretary: How do you spell it?

Jenson: C-R-U-Z.

Secretary: Great. Please come in for your interview.

Interviewer: Please introduce yourself to us.

Jenson: Good morning, sirs. My name is Jenson Cruz. I am 21 years old. I graduated from Chicago University. I majored in international finance at the department of Economy of the school. And I acquired the certificate of accountant in New York.

Interviewer: Okay, why did you apply for our company?

Jenson: Simpson inc. is leading the field of corporate finance in the world. I want to work as an accountant in that field.

Interviewer: Okay, You are one of the qualified applicants. Good luck to you.

Basic Expressions

a. I came here for my job interview.

b. I majored in international finance.

c. Why did you apply for our company?

Further Expressions

a. We'll look over your application.

b. What are job requirements of your company?

c. Our company recruits skilled personnel in Big Data.

d. What qualification does your company require?

Review 14-1 A

1. **Choose the correct one for the blank.**
I came here_____ my job interview.

a) for
b) with
c) on
d) at

2. **Choose the correct one for the blank.**
It ___ leading the field of international finance.

a) were
b) is
c) has
d) have

3. **Choose the one which is not appropriate for the blank.**
You are one of the qualified _______.

a) personnel
b) students
c) applicants
d) person

4. **Choose the correct one for the blank.**
Why did you ______ for our company?

a) applicant
b) apply
c) application
d) applied

Review 14-1 B

1. **Choose the correct one for the blank.**
We'll ______ your application.

a) looks
b) look
c) looking
d) look over

2. **Choose the correct one for the blank.**
What are job ________ of your company?

a) require
b) requirements
c) requires
d) requiring

3. **Choose the correct one for the blank.**
The interviewer works for the department of ______.

a) personnel
b) students
c) applicants
d) person

4. **Choose the correct one for the blank.**
Are you a/an ______ for our company?

a) applicant
b) apply
c) application
d) applied

Talk 14-2

Interviewer: Good morning, please introduce yourself, Mr. Jenson Cruz.

Jenson: Thank you very much for the opportunity for the job interview. I am Jenson Cruz. I am a student at the department of business adminstration of Hankuk College.

Interviewer: Do you have any experience of part- time job?

Jenson: Yes, I do. I worked part-time job for my tuition and living expenses.

Interviewer: What kind of part-time job did you have?

Jenson: I worked as an English interpreter for the foreign investors to Korean companies.

Interviewer: How was it?

Jenson: It was well paid. I loved it. But, frankly speaking, I want to have a more stable job like your company.

Interviewer: You look very honest. Thank you for the interview. Good luck to you.

Basic Expressions

a. Do you have any experience of part- time job?
b. I worked as an English interpreter.
c. I want to have a more stable job.

Further Expressions

a. The biggest problem for interviewees is speech.
b. They will interview you in depth.
c. He was nervous around the clock before a job interview.
d. The managing director is my supervisor.

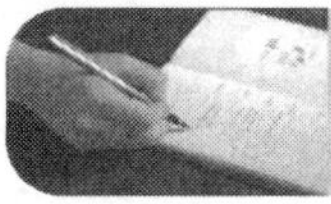

Review 14-2 A

1. **Choose the correct one for the blank.**
Thank you very much for the ________.

a) opportunity
b) stable
c) paid
d) invest

2. **Choose the correct one for the blank.**
I worked _____ an English interpreter.

a) on
b) at
c) to
d) as

3. **Choose the one which is not appropriate for the blank.**
_________, I want to have a good job from your company.

a) Frankly speaking
b) To be honest
c) Honestly
d) Honest

4. **Choose the correct one for the blank.**
Jane wants to have a more _______ job, due to her sick baby.

a) street
b) star
c) stable
d) start

Review 14–2 B

1. **Choose the correct one for the blank.**
The biggest problem for _______ is speech.

a) interviewees
b) internal
c) intra
d) intrigue

2. **Choose the correct one for the blank.**
The interviewers will interview you in ______.

a) dear
b) deer
c) deep
d) depth

3. **Choose the correct one for the blank.**
He was nervous around the _____ before a job interview.

a) click
b) clock
c) cloth
d) clear

4. **Choose the correct one for the blank.**
The managing director is my ________.

a) steep
b) supervisor
c) super
d) start

Scene 15 Weather

Talk 15-1

Jenson: It's a beautiful day, isn't it?

Amy: Yes. I like the clear weather.

Jenson: How was the weather yesterday? I came home from my business trip yesterday.

Amy: It rained cats and dogs. The torrential rain brought a disaster to the farmers.

Jenson: That's too bad. I am afraid that farmers are suffering from the disastrous weather.

Amy: A weather forecaster says it is expected to rain heavily again tomorrow.

Jenson: I am sorry to hear that. I would rather cancel going camping to Gangwon Province with my family.

Amy: You are right. You should be careful with the harsh weather these days.

Basic Expressions

a. I came home from my business trip.
b. It rained cats and dogs.
c. You should be careful with harsh weather.

Further Expressions

a. A meteorologist is expecting a hurricane
b. The typhoon caused a serious damage throughout the country
c. A blizzard is a long and intense snow storm
d. A weather forecaster says it is expected to rain heavily

Review 15-1 A

1. **Choose the correct one for the blank.**
I came home ______ my business trip.

a) to
b) from
c) at
d) on

2. **Choose the correct one for the blank.**
I am afraid ____ farmers are suffering from bad weather.

a) by
b) that
c) into
d) at

3. **Choose the one which is not appropriate for the blank.**
I am ______ to hear that.

a) sorry
b) happy
c) pleased
d) wonderful

4. **Choose the correct one for the blank.**
You should _____ careful with harsh weather.

a) are
b) be
c) is
d) were

Review 15-1 B

1. **Choose the correct one for the blank.**
A weather forecaster says it is expected to rain ______.

a) heaviness
b) heavily
c) heat
d) heating

2. **Choose the correct one for the blank.**
A meteorologist is __________ a hurricane.

a) expect
b) expects
c) expecting
d) expecter

3. **Choose the one which is not appropriate for the blank.**
A blizzard is a long and _______ snow storm.

a) heavy
b) intense
c) dreadful
d) warm

4. **Choose the correct one for the blank.**
The typhoon ______ a serious damage throughout the country.

a) causeful
b) causing
c) cause
d) caused

Talk 15-2

Jenson: The weather forecast has been unreliable these days.

Amy: You are right. It is because of changeable weather.

Jenson: Why is the weather so changeable and unpredictable?

Amy: Climate has been changed dramatically these days. Additionally climate change is a serious problem.

Jenson: I know your point. But I am asking you why it is so changeable.

Amy: That is because of El Nino and La Nina. They are affecting the weather temperatures around the world.

Jenson: I see. I heard that the butterfly effect has been originated from the weather.

Amy: You are right. The butterfly effect theory was created by an American meteorologist, Edward Norton Lorenz in 1961.

Jenson: Wow, you must be a Mr. Know-It-All.

Basic Expressions

a. The weather forecast has been unreliable these days.
b. They are affecting the weather temperatures around the world.
c. Butterfly effect theory was created by an American meteorologist.

Further Expressions

a. The average seawater temperature increased around 1 degree in a decade.
b. The seawater temperature has been on the rise.
c. You must be a Mr. Know-It-All.
d. The greenhouse effect is a serious problem.

Review 15-2 A

1. **Choose the correct one for the blank.**
The weather forecast has ______ unreliable these days.

a) is
b) was
c) be
d) been

2. **Choose the correct one for the blank.**
They are ______ the weather temperatures around the world.

a) affecting
b) affects
c) effect
d) effects

3. **Choose the one which is not appropriate for the blank.**
I ______ you why it is so changeable.

a) am asking
b) ask
c) asks
d) have been asking

4. **Choose the correct one for the blank.**
Butterfly effect theory was ______ by an American meteorologist.

a) creation
b) creates
c) creator
d) created

Review 15–2 B

1. **Choose the correct one for the blank.**
The average seawater temperature ______ around 1 degree in a decade.

a) increasable
b) incredible
c) increasing
d) increased

2. **Choose the correct one for the blank.**
The weather temperature has been _____ the rise.

a) to
b) on
c) with
d) within

3. **Choose the one which is not appropriate for the blank.**
The greenhouse effect is a ________ problem.

a) dreadful
b) disastrous
c) beneficial
d) serious

4. **Choose the correct one for the blank.**
He must _____ a Mr. Know–It–All.

a) are
b) is
c) was
d) be

〈해설 및 정답 편〉

Scene 1 How are you?

Talk 1-1

Amy: Hi. How are you?

에이미: 안녕, 어떻게 지내?

Kevin: I'm very good. How are you ?

케빈: 아주 좋아. 넌 어때?

Amy: I'm so good, too.

에이미: 나도 좋아.

Amy: It's a great day, isn't it?

에이미: 좋은 날씨인데, 그렇지?

Kevin: Yes it is. I really love sunny days.

케빈: 맞아. 난 햇볕이 드는 날이 좋아.

Amy: Do you? I am happy you like sunny days like me.

에이미: 그래? 네가 나처럼 햇볕 드는 날씨를 좋아해서 좋네.

Kevin: Oh, it's already ten to 9.

케빈: 오, 벌써 9시 10분전이다.

I'd better get going right now for the class. See you soon.

수업 때문에 가봐야겠다. 곧 보자.

Amy: Bye, see you tomorrow.

에이미: 안녕, 내일 보자

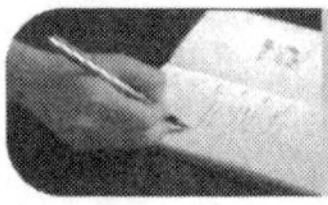

Review 1-1 A

1. Choose the correct one for the blank.
(빈칸에 맞는 표현을 고르시오.)

How ___ you?
(어떻게 지내니?)

a) are
b) is
c) has
d) have

정답 **a)**

2. Choose the correct one for the blank.
(빈칸에 맞는 표현을 고르시오.)

I'd better ______ going right now.
(지금 가는게 더 좋겠다.)

a) gets
b) getting
c) get
d) got

정답 **c)**

3. Choose the one which is not appropriate for the blank.
(빈칸에 알맞지 않는 표현을 고르시오.)

See you ________

a) tomorrow
b) next time
c) later
d) not

정답 **d)**

4. Choose the one which is not appropriate for the blank.
(빈칸에 알맞지 않는 표현을 고르시오.)

I really ______ sunny days.

a) like
b) love
c) hate
d) do

정답 **d)**

Review 1-1 B

1. **Choose the correct one for the blank.**
(빈칸에 맞는 표현을 고르시오.)

How _____ you been these days?
(요즘 어떻게 지내요?)

a) have
b) is
c) has
d) are

정답 **a)**

2. **Choose the correct one for the blank.**
(빈칸에 맞는 표현을 고르시오.)

The weather is so nice, and it couldn't be ______.
(날씨가 아주 좋다, 더할 나위 없이 좋다.)

a) bat
b) bet
c) batter
d) better

정답 **d)**

3. Choose the one which is not appropriate for the blank.
(빈칸에 알맞지 않는 표현을 고르시오.)

It's already ________to ten.

a) a quarter
b) ten
c) five
d) second

정답 d)

4 Choose the correct one for the blank.
(빈칸에 맞는 표현을 고르시오.)

See you in the ______ future.
(가까운 미래에 봅시다.)

a) now
b) nearby
c) nest
d) near

정답 d)

Talk 1-2.

Kevin: Hi, Amy. How are you?

케빈: 안녕, 에이미, 어떻게 지내?

Amy: Fine, thanks. Kevin, this is Lisa.

에이미: 좋아, 캐빈, 이쪽은 리사야.

Kevin: Hello, Lisa.

케빈: 안녕, 리사

Lisa: How do you do?

리사: 처음 뵙겠습니다

Kevin: How do you do?

케빈: 처음 뵙겠습니다

Lisa: Nice to meet you.

리사: 만나서 반가워요

Kevin: Nice to meet you, too.

케빈: 저도 만나서 반가워요

Kevin: Lisa, where are you from?

케빈: 리사, 어디서 왔어요?

Lisa: I'm from New Zealand.

리사: 뉴질랜드에서 왔어요.

Kevin: Are you here on vacation?

케빈: 여기 휴가차 왔나요?

Lisa: No. I'm here on business for a movie.

리사: 아니요. 영화 사업차 왔어요.

Kevin: What do you do?

케빈: 어떤 일 하시는지요?

Lisa: I'm a movie promoter.

리사: 영화 프로모터입니다.

Lisa: Kevin, what do you do?

리사: 캐빈, 어떤 일을 하시나요?

Kevin: I'm a professional baseball player.

케빈: 저는 프로야구 선수입니다.

Review 1-2 A

1. **Choose the correct one for the blank.**
(빈칸에 맞는 표현을 고르시오.)

How are you ______ ?
(어떻게 지내요?)

a) do
b) does
c) doing
d) done

정답 **c)**

2 **Choose the correct one for the blank.**
(빈칸에 맞는 표현을 고르시오.)

What is your ________?
(직업이 무엇이죠?)

a) occupy
b) occupant
c) occupied
d) occupation

정답 **d)**

3 **Choose the one which is not appropriate for the blank.**
(빈칸에 알맞지 않는 표현을 고르시오.)

A: What do you do? (직업이 무엇입니까?)

B: ________________

a) I'm a movie star (영화 배우입니다)
b) My job is a teacher (직업이 선생님입니다)
c) I sleep late at night (밤에 늦게 잡니다)
d) I deliver goods to the clerks. (점원들에게 물건을 배달합니다)

정답 **c)**

4 **Choose the one which is not appropriate for the blank.**
(빈칸에 알맞지 않는 표현을 고르시오.)

A: I'm ______ to meet you.

a) glad
b) happy
c) pleased
d) well

정답 **d)**

Review 1–2 B

1. **Choose the correct one for the blank.**
(빈칸에 알맞은 표현을 고르시오.)

What do you do for a _______?
(생계를 위해 무엇을 하나요?)

a) living
b) live
c) lives
d) liver

정답 **a)**

2. **Choose the correct one for the blank.**
(빈칸에 알맞은 표현을 고르시오.)

I'm here _____ business.
(저는 사업차 여기 왔습니다.)

a) by
b) on
c) with
d) over

정답 **b)**

3. Choose the one which is not appropriate for the blank.
(빈칸에 알맞지 않은 표현을 고르시오.)

______ I ask what your occupation is?

a) May
b) Can
c) Do you mind if
d) When do

정답 **d)**

4. Choose the correct one for the blank.
(빈칸에 알맞은 표현을 고르시오.)

You can't ______ what your occupation is
(당신은 직업을 감출 수 없습니다)

a) hide
b) hidden
c) hides
d) hiding

정답 **a)**

Scene 2 Where do you work?

Talk 2-1

Kevin: Where do you work?

케빈: 어디서 일하니?

Amy: I work for Korean Air.

에이미: 대한항공에서 일해요.

Kevin: Oh, do you?

케빈: 오, 그래요?

Kevin: What do you do for Korean Air?

케빈: 대한항공에서 어떤 일을 하나요?

Amy: I work as a stewardess.

에이미: 승무원으로 일해요.

Amy: Where do you work, Kavin?

에이미: 어디서 일하니, 캐빈?

Kevin: I work for the Korean government.

케빈: 한국 정부를 위해 일해요.

Amy: What do you mean by that?

에이미: 무슨 뜻이죠?

Kevin: I am a public official.

케빈: 공무원입니다.

Review 2-1 A

1. Choose the correct one for the blank.
(빈칸에 맞는 표현을 고르시오.)

Where do you ______ ?
(어디 사십니까?)

a) work
b) works
c) working
d) worked

정답 a)

2. Choose the correct one for the blank.
(빈칸에 맞는 표현을 고르시오.)

I work ______ Johnson and Johnson Inc.
(저는 존슨앤 존슨 회사를 위해 일합니다.)

a) by
b) on
c) for
d) to

정답 c)

3. **Choose the correct one for the blank.**
(빈칸에 맞는 표현을 고르시오.)

Janet is a great flight ______ as I know.
(자넷은 제가 알기로는 훌륭한 승무원입니다.)

a) attending
b) attend
c) attendant
d) attendants

정답 **c)**

4. **Choose the correct one for the blank.**
(빈칸에 맞는 표현을 고르시오.)

My supervisor is in _____of the planning department.
(나의 상사는 기획부서에 책임을 지고 있다.)

a) chance
b) charge
c) change
d) champion

정답 **b)**

Review 2-1 B

1. **Choose the correct one for the blank.**
(빈칸에 맞는 표현을 고르시오.)

She is a member of cabin _____ for Korean Air.
(그녀는 대한항공의 승무원의 일원이다.)

a) crew
b) cross
c) creek
d) cliff

정답 **a)**

2. **Choose the correct one for the blank.**
(빈칸에 맞는 표현을 고르시오.)

He is a high-level official ___ the diplomatic department.
(그는 외교 부서에 있는 고위급 관료이다.)

a) by
b) on
c) in
d) to

정답 **c)**

3. **Choose the correct one for the blank.**
(빈칸에 맞는 표현을 고르시오.)

Jane's father is a public _______ for the government.
(자넷의 아버지는 정부 공무원이다.)

a) offer
b) office
c) official
d) offering

정답 **c)**

4. **Choose the correct one for the blank.**
(빈칸에 맞는 표현을 고르시오.)

What do you mean ______?
(무슨 말씀인가요?)

a) by those
b) by that
c) by us
d) by ours

정답 **b)**

Talk 2-2

Jenson: What are you doing now?

젠슨: 지금 무슨 일을 하나요?

Kevin: I'm searching for a book about 3D printers.

케빈: 3 D 프린터에 관련된 책을 찾고 있습니다.

Jenson: I'll buy a book on 3 D printers tomorrow.

젠슨: 내일 3 D 프린터에 관련된 책을 살 것입니다.

Kevin: What did you say?

케빈: 무슨 말씀이시죠?

Jenson: I'll buy a book on 3 D printers.

젠슨: 3 D 프린터에 관련된 책을 살 것입니다.

Kevin: Really? Are you sure of the future of 3 D printers?

케빈: 정말요? 3 D 프린터의 미래에 대해서 확신하시나요?

Jenson: Of course, would you give me some tips about 3 D printers?

젠슨: 물론이죠, 3 D 프린터에 관련된 조언을 좀 해주실래요?

Kevin: Ok, let me give you some.

케빈: 좋아요, 좀 해드리지요.

Review 2-2 A

1. **Choose the correct one for the blank.**
(빈칸에 맞는 표현을 고르시오.)

I am_______ for the business books for my homework.
(저는 숙제를 위해 비즈니스 서적을 찾는 중입니다.)

a) searches
b) searcher
c) searching
d) search

정답 **c)**

2. **Choose the correct one for the blank.**
(빈칸에 맞는 표현을 고르시오.)

I'll buy a book _______3 D printers.
(나는 3 D 프린터에 관한 책을 살 것이다.)

a) by
b) on
c) at
d) to

정답 **b)**

3. **Choose the correct one for the blank.**
(빈칸에 맞는 표현을 고르시오.)

Let me ______ you some good tips.
(좋은 조언을 해드리도록 하죠.)

a) given
b) gives
c) give
d) giver

정답 **c)**

4. **Choose the correct one for the blank.**
(빈칸에 맞는 표현을 고르시오.)

Are you _____ of what you are talking to me?
(당신은 나에게 말한 것을 확신합니까?)

a) assurance
b) sure
c) such
d) surfing

정답 **b)**

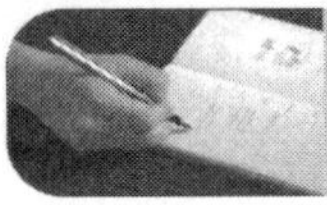

Review 2-2 B

1. **Choose the correct one for the blank.**
(빈칸에 맞는 표현을 고르시오.)

I'm in ______ of the books on Industrial Revolution.
(나는 산업 혁명에 관한 책을 찾고 있다.)

a) search
b) searching
c) searches
d) searcher

정답 **a)**

2. **Choose the correct one for the blank.**
(빈칸에 맞는 표현을 고르시오.)

Let me _______ a good tablet computer.
(좋은 테블릿 컴퓨터를 살려고 해요.)

a) purchases
b) purchasing
c) purchase
d) purchaser

정답 **c)**

3. **Choose the correct one for the blank.**
(빈칸에 맞는 표현을 고르시오.)

You need good tips ____ how to study English.

a) between
b) at
c) on
d) beneath

정답 **c)**

4. **Choose the correct one for the blank.**
(빈칸에 맞는 표현을 고르시오.)

3 D printers can produce three __________ objects.
(3 D 프린터는 3차원의 물체를 생산할 수 있다.)

a) dimension
b) dimensional
c) dimensions
d) dimensionals

정답 **b)**

Scene 3 Thank you for the invitation

Talk 3-1

Amy: Hi, Lisa. How have you been?

에이미: 안녕, 리사. 어떻게 지내?

Lisa: Fine, thanks. Please make yourself comfortable.

리사: 좋아. 편히 지내길.

Lisa: Lunch will be ready soon. Take a seat.

리사: 점심이 곧 준비될거야. 앉아.

Amy: Oh, how kind you are. Thank you for your invitation to lunch.

에이미: 오, 친절하기도 하지. 점심식사 초대해 줘서 고마워.

Lisa: Please, help yourself.

리사: 마음껏 드세요.

Amy: Thanks a lot, your pasta is delicious.

에이미: 고마워, 네가 해준 파스타 맛있네.

Lisa: Would you like some more pasta?

리사: 파스타 더 먹을래?

Amy: Oh, yes, please. And may I have one more glass of soft drink?

에이미: 오, 좋죠. 그리고 청량음료 한잔 더 해도 될까요?

Lisa: With my pleasure, here you are.

리사: 당연하죠, 여깄어요.

Amy: Wow, you must be an excellent cook.

에이미: 와우, 너는 훌륭한 요리사임에 틀림없다.

Lisa: Thank you for your compliment.

리사: 칭찬해주어 고마워.

Review 3-1 A

1. **Choose the correct one for the blank.**
(빈칸에 맞는 표현을 고르시오.)

Would you _______ some more food?
(음식 더 드시겠습니까?)

a) liked
b) likes
c) like
d) liking

정답 c)

2. **Choose the correct one for the blank.**
(빈칸에 맞는 표현을 고르시오.)

Please make yourself _________.
(편히 지내십시오.)

a) at house
b) at home
c) at desk
d) at night

정답 b)

3. **Choose the correct one for the blank.**
(빈칸에 맞는 표현을 고르시오.)

We prepared various kinds of food. ______ yourself.
(우리가 많은 음식을 준비했어요. 마음껏 드세요.)

a) Hell
b) Help
c) Hello
d) Hull

정답 **b)**

4. **Choose the correct one for the blank.**
(빈칸에 맞는 표현을 고르시오.)

Please, take a ______ for your lunch.
(점심식사를 위해 의자에 앉으세요.)

a) seats
b) sit down
c) sit
d) seat

정답 **d)**

Review 3-1 B

1. Choose the correct one for the blank.
(빈칸에 맞는 표현을 고르시오.)

To have a party _____ a lot of fun.
(파티하는 것은 많이 재미있다.)

a) been
b) is
c) does
d) be

정답 **b)**

2. Choose the correct one for the blank.
(빈칸에 맞는 표현을 고르시오.)

The restaurant uses _____ ingredients for Pizza.
(이 식당은 피자를 위해 신선한 재료를 사용한다.)

a) fresh
b) freight
c) free
d) fraud

정답 **a)**

3. **Choose the correct one for the blank.**
(빈칸에 맞는 표현을 고르시오.)

Mr. Kim likes to ______ for himself.
(미스터 김은 자신이 요리하는 것을 좋아해.)

a) cook
b) cooker
c) cooking
d) cooked

정답 **a)**

4. **Choose the correct one for the blank.**
(빈칸에 맞는 표현을 고르시오.)

Your food is great and nothing to be _______.
(너의 음식은 훌륭해서 발랄것이 없다.)

a) desirous
b) desires
c) desire
d) desired

정답 **d)**

Talk 3-2

Jenson: Thank you for the invitation to your housewarming.

젠슨: 집들이에 초대해 주어 고마워요.

Kevin: The pleasure is mine.

케빈: 제가 기쁜걸요.

Kevin: Have you ever tried spicy Korean food?

케빈: 매운 한국 음식 먹어본적 있니?

Jenson: Yes, I love eating Tteokbokki. In other word, stir-fried rice cake in Korea, it's very hot.

젠슨: 네, 저는 떡볶기 먹는 것을 좋아해요. 즉, 한국의 볶은 쌀 케익이죠. 매워요.

Kevin: Well, you are right. To soothe the spicy taste some Koreans enjoy soup of fish cake together.

맞아요. 매운 맛을 달래기 위해서 한국사람들은 어묵 국물을 함께 즐겨요.

Jenson: You must be really busy preparing food for the party.

젠슨: 파티용 음식 준비하느라 네가 정말 바쁘구나.

Kevin: My wife and I did our best to make homemade Tteokbokki.

케빈: 내 아내와 나는 가정용 떡볶기 만드느라 최선을 다했어.

Jenson: It is so hot! But it's tasty.

젠슨: 매워! 하지만 맛있어.

Kevin: Thank you, please help yourself and also make yourself at home.

케빈: 고마워, 마음껏 먹고 편히 지내.

Review 3-2 A

1. **Choose the correct one for the blank.**
(빈칸에 맞는 표현을 고르시오.)

You must ___ really busy preparing food for the party.
(너는 파티를 위한 음식을 준비하느라 바쁨에 틀림없다.)

a) been
b) do
c) be
d) is

정답 c)

2. **Choose the correct one for the blank.**
(빈칸에 맞는 표현을 고르시오.)

Have you ever _____ spicy food?
(매운 음식 먹어본적 있나요?)

a) tries
b) try
c) tried
d) trying

정답 c)

3. **Choose the correct one for the blank.**
(빈칸에 맞는 표현을 고르시오.)

Thank you for your ______ to lunch.
(점심식사에 초대해 주어 고마워요.)

a) invite
b) invitation
c) invites
d) invitational

정답 **b)**

4. **Choose the one which is not appropriate for the blank.**
(빈칸에 알맞지 않는 표현을 고르시오.)

I really appreciate your ________ food for my birthday.

a) delicious
b) tasty
c) terrible
d) yummy

정답 **c)**

Review 3-2 B

1. **Choose the correct one for the blank.**
(빈칸에 맞는 표현을 고르시오.)

Homemade food is healthier _____ the restaurant food.
(가정에서 만든 음식이 식당음식보다 더 건강하다.)

a) then
b) that
c) than
d) this

정답 c)

2. **Choose the correct one for the blank.**
(빈칸에 맞는 표현을 고르시오.)

She did her best to _____ healthy food.
(그녀는 건강한 음식을 만들기 위해 최선을 다했다.)

a) come
b) go
c) make
d) do

정답 c)

3. **Choose the correct one for the blank.**
(빈칸에 맞는 표현을 고르시오.)

They put their ____ into a meal for the baby.
(그들은 아기를 위한 음식을 만드느라 정열을 쏟았다.)

a) heal
b) heart
c) hit
d) brain

정답 **b)**

4. **Choose the correct one for the blank.**
(빈칸에 맞는 표현을 고르시오.)

People say that _______ is the best source.
(사람들은 시장이 반찬이라고 한다.)

a) hunk
b) hungary
c) hungry
d) hunger

정답 **d)**

Scene 4 What can I do for you?

Talk 4-1

Clerk: What can I do for you?

점원: 무엇을 도와드릴까요?

Lisa: Good evening. I'm looking for a T-shirt.

리사: 안녕하세요. 티셔츠를 찾고 있습니다.

Clerk: What color do you want?

점원: 어떤 색을 원하시나요?

Lisa: Red.

리사: 빨간색이요.

Clerk: And what kind of design do you want?

점원: 그리고 어떤 종류의 디자인을 원하시나요?

Lisa: I'm not sure.

리사: 확실치 않네요.

Clerk: How about this shirt?

점원: 이 셔츠는 어때요?

Lisa: Oh, it looks good. Can I try it on?

리사: 오, 좋아 보이네요. 입어봐도 되나요?

Clerk: Sure, you can.

점원: 물론이죠, 입어보실수 있어요.

Lisa: Thank you.

리사: 고마워요.

Lisa: How much does it cost?

리사: 얼마인가요?

Clerk: Forty thousand won.

점원: 4만원입니다.

Lisa: It sounds reasonable. Let me buy it.

리사: 괜찮네요. 사도록 하죠.

Clerk: Thank you for your purchase.

점원: 구매후 주셔서 감사합니다.

Review 4-1 A

1. **Choose the correct one for the blank.**
(빈칸에 알맞은 표현을 고르시오.)

How ______ I help you?
(어떻게 도와드릴까요?)

a) been
b) done
c) may
d) am

정답 c)

2. **Choose the correct one for the blank.**
(빈칸에 알맞은 표현을 고르시오.)

The T-shirt ______ great on you.
(티셔츠가 당신에게는 멋져 보입니다.)

a) lookers
b) looking
c) looks
d) looker

정답 c)

3. **Choose the one which is not appropriate for the blank.**
(빈칸에 알맞지 않는 표현을 고르시오.)

My friend _______ a famous designer in the fashion industry.

a) is
b) are
c) has been
d) was

정답 **b)**

4. **Choose the correct one for the blank.**
(빈칸에 알맞은 표현을 고르시오.)

She is looking _____ cheaper shirts to save living cost.
(그녀는 생활비를 줄이기 위해 싼 셔츠를 찾는 중입니다.)

a) to
b) for
c) through
d) by

정답 **b)**

Review 4-1 B

1. **Choose the correct one for the blank.**
(빈칸에 알맞은 표현을 고르시오.)

Can I try it _____ ?
(제가 입어봐도 되나요?)

a) over
b) on
c) to
d) before

정답 **b)**

2. **Choose the correct one for the blank.**
(빈칸에 알맞은 표현을 고르시오.)

Mrs. Peterson works in the _____ department.
(페터슨씨는 영업부에서 일한다.)

a) sell
b) sale
c) sales
d) sells

정답 **c)**

3. **Choose the correct one for the blank.**
(빈칸에 알맞은 표현을 고르시오.)

How about _______ this T- shirt?
(이 셔츠 고르는 것은 어때?)

a) choosing
b) choice
c) choices
d) chosen

정답 **a)**

4. **Choose the correct one for the blank.**
(빈칸에 알맞은 표현을 고르시오.)

The fashion outlet is having a _______ sale.
(그 의류 아울렛은 재고정리 세일을 한다.)

a) clarified
b) clearance
c) clarity
d) cliff

정답 **b)**

Talk 4-2

Lisa: Let me buy a back pack. How much is this?

리사: 가방을 사려고 합니다. 얼마지요?

Clerk: Good evening, it is normally one hundred dollars. But it is on sale for sixty dollars.

점원: 안녕하세요, 보통 백달러입니다. 하지만 60달러에 할인하고 있습니다.

Lisa: It sounds good. Do you have other back packs on sale?

리사: 좋아요. 싸게 파는 다른 가방 있나요?

Clerk: Sure. We have a variety of new back packs on sale on the second floor.

점원: 물론이죠. 2층에 할인하는 다양한 새로운 가방들이 있습니다.

Lisa: OK. Let me go upstairs.

리사: 좋아요. 윗층으로 가보죠.

Clerk: You can use the escalator over there.

점원: 저기 에스컬레이터를 이용하실 수 있습니다.

Lisa: Which day is the last of the sale?

리사: 세일 마지막 날이 언제인가요?

Clerk: Tomorrow is the last day. Thank you.

점원: 내일이 마지막 날입니다. 고맙습니다.

Review 4-2 A

1. **Choose the correct one for the blank.**
(빈칸에 맞는 표현을 고르시오.)

_______ can I do for you?
(무엇을 도와드릴까요?)

a) What
b) Who
c) Where
d) Whose

정답 a)

2. **Choose the correct one for the blank.**
(빈칸에 맞는 표현을 고르시오.)

Do you have back packs _____ sale?
(가방 싸게 팝니까?)

a) with
b) in
c) on
d) over

정답 c)

3. **Choose the correct one for the blank.**
(빈칸에 맞는 표현을 고르시오.)

The shop has a _______ of goods on sports.
(상점은 다양한 스포츠 용품이 있다.)

a) various
b) vary
c) variety
d) varying

정답 c)

4. **Choose the correct one for the blank.**
(빈칸에 맞는 표현을 고르시오.)

_______ me go upstairs for other goods.
(다른 상품을 위해 위로 가봅시다.)

a) Let's
b) Let us
c) Let
d) Lets

정답 c)

Review 4-2 B

1. **Choose the correct one for the blank.**
(빈칸에 맞는 표현을 고르시오.)

A: How much is this back pack?
(이 가방 얼마입니까?)

B: It will cost ______ eighty thousand one.
(8만원입니다.)

a) you
b) yours
c) you're
d) your

정답 **a)**

2. **Choose the correct one for the blank.**
(빈칸에 맞는 표현을 고르시오.)

She wants to buy her new mobile phone ________ of expense.
(그녀는 경비와 상관없이 새로운 휴대폰을 구매하기를 원한다.)

a) regarding
b) regard
c) regardless
d) regards

정답 **c)**

3. **Choose the correct one for the blank.**
(빈칸에 맞는 표현을 고르시오.)

The boss of the company restricts ________ on paper consumption.
(회사의 사장은 종이 소비에 대한 지출을 제한한다.)

a) express
b) extra
c) expenditure
d) exclusive

정답 **c)**

4. **Choose the correct one for the blank.**
(빈칸에 맞는 표현을 고르시오.)

Save _______ money for your future.
(당신의 미래를 위해서 여분의 돈을 모으시오.)

a) extreme
b) active
c) extra
d) acute

정답 **c)**

Scene 5 What would you like to order?

Talk 5-1

Server: Can I take your order, sir?

서버: 주문 받아도 될까요, 선생님?

Jenson: What is the popular dish at this restaurant?

젠슨: 이 레스토랑의 인기있는 음식이 뭐죠?

Server: The T-bone steak is the most popular menu.

서버: T본 스테이크가 가장 인기 있습니다.

Jenson: And then, let me have a T-bone steak.

젠슨: 그러면, T본 스테이크를 먹도록 하죠.

Server: How would you like your steak, sir?

서버: 스테이크 굽기 어떻게 해드릴까요, 선생님?

Jenson: Rare, please.

젠슨: 설익혀 주세요.

Server: Do you need anything to drink?

서버: 마실 것이 필요하신가요?

Jenson: A glass of orange juice with ice, please.

젠슨: 얼음 넣은 오렌지 쥬스로 해주세요.

Server: Let me serve you right away with what you have ordered.

서버: 주문하신 것으로 곧 모시도록 하겠습니다.

Jenson: Thank you.

젠슨: 고마워요.

Review 5-1 A

1. **Choose the correct one for the blank.**
(빈칸에 맞는 표현을 고르시오.)

Do you mind if I _____ your order?
(주문 받아도 되겠습니까?)

a) taking
b) taken
c) take
d) takes

정답 **c)**

2. **Choose the correct one for the blank.**
(빈칸에 맞는 표현을 고르시오.)

How would you ______ your steak?
(스테이크 어떻게 해드릴까요?)

a) likes
b) like
c) liking
d) liked

정답 **b)**

3. **Choose the one which is not appropriate for the blank.**
(빈칸에 알맞지 않는 표현을 고르시오.)

A: Do you need anything to drink?
(마실 것이 필요하십니까?)

B: ________________

a) A glass of wine, please
b) A can of seven-up, please
c) A bottle of mineral water, please
d) A piece of blanket, please

정답 **d)**

4. **Choose the correct one for the blank.**
(빈칸에 맞는 표현을 고르시오.)

In _____ to lose weight, she works out everyday.
(체중을 줄이기 위해서 그녀는 매일 운동한다.)

a) have
b) order
c) take
d) go

정답 **b)**

Review 5-1 B

1. **Choose the correct one for the blank.**
(빈칸에 맞는 표현을 고르시오.)

She is ____ a diet, since she wants to look slim.
(그녀는 날씬해 보이고 싶어서 다이어트를 한다.)

a) to
b) over
c) on
d) between

정답 **c)**

2. **Choose the correct one for the blank.**
(빈칸에 맞는 표현을 고르시오.)

Her religion ________ dietary control.
(그녀의 종료는 음식통제를 요구한다.)

a) demand
b) demands
c) demanding
d) to demand

정답 **b)**

3. **Choose the correct one for the blank.**
(빈칸에 맞는 표현을 고르시오.)

You should not eat food ______ at night if you are on a diet.
(당신은 다이어트 중 일때는 밤늦게 음식을 먹어서는 안된다.)

a) little
b) least
c) last
d) late

정답 **d)**

4. **Choose the correct one for the blank.**
(빈칸에 맞는 표현을 고르시오.)

I eat less and work out on a regular ______.
(나는 적게 먹고 규칙적으로 운동한다.)

a) base
b) bat
c) best
d) basis

정답 **d)**

Talk 5-2

Server: What would you like to order, sir?

서버: 무엇을 준비하시겠습니까, 선생님?

Jenson: Let me have a slice of potato pizza and a can of coke.

젠슨: 포테이토 피자와 콜라 한캔이요.

Jenson: What would you like to have, Amy?

젠슨: 무엇을 먹고 싶니, 에이미?

Amy: Let me take a look at the menu.

에이미: 메뉴를 봅시다.

Server: Cheese pizza is the specialty at our restaurant.

서버: 치즈 피자는 우리 식당의 특별 요리에요.

Amy: Why your cheese pizza is special?

에이미: 왜 치즈 피자가 특별한가요?

Server: We import fresh and gourmet cheese from the local farms in France directly.

서버: 우리는 신선하고 맛있는 치즈를 프랑스 지역 농장에서 직접 수입합니다.

Amy: It sounds good. Let me try cheese pizza.

에이미: 좋아요. 치즈 피자를 먹어보죠.

Server: Will you have a drink?

서버: 음료를 드시겠습니까?

Amy: Yes, a glass of sprite, but without ice.

에이미: 네, 스프라이트 한잔이요, 하지만 얼음과 함께요.

Server: I see, ma'am. Let me serve you soon with your food.

서버: 네, 선생님. 음식과 함께 곧 모시겠습니다.

Amy: Thank you for your kindness.

에이미: 친절함에 감사드려요.

Review 5-2 A

1. **Choose the correct one for the blank.**
(빈칸에 맞는 표현을 고르시오.)

Can I take your _____ ?
(주문 받아도 될까요?)

a) ordering
b) ordered
c) order
d) to order

정답 **c)**

2. **Choose the correct one for the blank.**
(빈칸에 맞는 표현을 고르시오.)

Cheese pizza is the ________ at this restaurant.
(치즈 피자는 이 식당에서 특별품이다.)

a) special
b) specialty
c) specialize
d) specialized

정답 **b)**

3. **Choose the one which is not appropriate for the blank.**
(빈칸에 알맞지 않는 표현을 고르시오.)

A: What would you like to order?
(무엇을 주문하시겠습니까?)

B: ________________

a) A glass of wine, please
b) A slice of pizza
c) Rare, please
d) Firstly, let me take a look at the menu.

정답 **c)**

4. **Choose the one which is not appropriate for the blank.**
(빈칸에 알맞지 않는 표현을 고르시오.)

What would you like to ______?

a) have
b) order
c) take
d) go

정답 **d)**

Review 5-2 B

1. Choose the correct one for the blank.
(빈칸에 맞는 표현을 고르시오.)

Let me have a _______ of potato pizza.
(피자 한 조각 먹읍시다.)

a) slow
b) sleep
c) slice
d) slip

정답 **c)**

2. Choose the correct one for the blank.
(빈칸에 맞는 표현을 고르시오.)

She enjoys the ________ food at the restaurant.
(그녀는 맛있는 음식을 식당에서 즐긴다.)

a) gone
b) gourmet
c) ghost
d) go

정답 **b)**

3. **Choose the correct one for the blank.**
(빈칸에 맞는 표현을 고르시오.)

They ate shark's fin soup, a ______ in China.
(그들은 중국의 맛있는 요리인 샥스핀을 먹었다.)

a) deal
b) deliberate
c) delicacy
d) delight

정답 **c)**

4. **Choose the correct one for the blank.**
(빈칸에 맞는 표현을 고르시오.)

Food ______ is a serious disease during the summer season.
(식중독은 여름동안 심각한 질병이다.)

a) pottery
b) poem
c) post
d) poisoning

정답 **d)**

Scene 6 At the post office

Talk 6-1

Jenson: Good morning, I'd like to send this parcel by registered post.

젠슨: 좋은 아침입니다, 이 소포를 등기로 보내고 싶습니다.

Clerk: You have two options, by air or by sea.

직원: 선택사항이 두가지입니다, 항공편 혹은 배편입니다.

Jenson: By air please, and also by special delivery.

젠슨: 배편으로 부탁하구요, 그리고 속달로 해주세요.

Clerk: Is there anything valuable inside the parcel?

직원: 소포안에 귀중품 들어 있나요?

Jenson: Nothing valuable

젠슨: 귀중품 없습니다.

Clerk: Do you have any dangerous or illegal items in it?

직원: 안에 위험하거나 불법적인 것 있나요?

Jenson: Don't worry about it. It is just a book.

젠슨: 걱정마세요. 그냥 책입니다.

Clerk: Okay, it will be fifty five dollars.

직원: 좋아요, 50달러입니다.

Jenson: Can I use my credit card here?

젠슨: 여기서 신용카드 써도 되나요?

Clerk: No problem, sir.

직원: 문제없습니다, 선생님.

Review 6-1 A

1. **Choose the correct one for the blank.**
(빈칸에 맞는 표현을 고르시오.)

Let me ______ this letter by special mail?
(속달로 이 편지를 보냅시다.)

a) sending
b) sender
c) send
d) sends

정답 c)

2. **Choose the correct one for the blank.**
(빈칸에 맞는 표현을 고르시오.)

The postage of air mail is more ______ than that of regular mail.
(항공편 우표는 보통 우편보다 더 비싸다.)

a) extending
b) extend
c) expensive
d) expansion

정답 c)

3. **Choose the one which is not appropriate for the blank.**
(빈칸에 알맞지 않은 표현을 고르시오.)

Thank you for your ________.

a) advice
b) tips
c) kind
d) purchase

정답 c)

4. **Choose the correct one for the blank.**
(빈칸에 맞는 표현을 고르시오.)

________ requires to be adhered on the envelope.
(우표는 봉투에 붙여질 것이 요구됩니다.)

a) Post
b) Postage
c) Portal
d) Pork

정답 b)

Review 6-1 B

1. **Choose the correct one for the blank.**
(빈칸에 맞는 표현을 고르시오.)

How ____ is the nearest post office from here?
(여기서 가장 가까운 우체국이 어디죠?)

a) front
b) free
c) far
d) feeling

정답 c)

2. **Choose the correct one for the blank.**
(빈칸에 맞는 표현을 고르시오.)

Enter your zip code or _______ code for the address.
(주소를 위해 집코드 혹은 우편보호를 입력하세요.)

a) poster
b) posting
c) postal
d) position

정답 c)

3. **Choose the correct one for the blank.**
(빈칸에 맞는 표현을 고르시오.)

Any recipient should be ___ home at time of delivery.
(배달시에는 수령자가 집에 있어야 합니다.)

a) to
b) with
c) at
d) between

정답 **c)**

4. **Choose the correct one for the blank.**
(빈칸에 맞는 표현을 고르시오.)

How much will it cost to send this by________ mail?
(특급우편으로 보내려면 얼마나 드나요?)

a) night
b) over
c) overnight
d) day

정답 **c)**

Talk 6-2

Clerk: Next customer, please.

직원: 다음 손님 오세요.

Amy: Good afternoon, let me send this letter by air.

에이미: 안녕하세요, 이 편지를 항공편으로 보내려고 합니다.

Clerk: By registered mail or ordinary mail?

직원: 등기인가요 아니면 일반 우편인가요?

Amy: By ordinary mail, please.

에이미: 일반 우편으로 부탁드립니다.

Clerk: You should pay 24 dollars for it.

직원: 24달러를 직불하셔야 합니다.

Amy: Okay, let me see. I am searching for my wallet.

에이미: 좋아요, 그런데 내 지갑을 찾는 중입니다.

Clerk: Both cash and credit card will do. Will you pay by cash or credit card?

직원: 현금과 신용카드 둘다 됩니다. 현금으로 하실래요, 아니면 신용카드로 하실래요?

Amy: I don't carry any credit cards. Here is three ten-dollar bills.

에이미: 신용카드를 가지고 다니지 않습니다. 10달러짜리 지폐 3장이 있네요.

Clerk: Thank you. Take the postage and your change.

직원: 고맙습니다. 우표와 잔돈 가져가세요.

Amy: Oh, thank you. I appreciate your kindness.

에이미: 오, 고마워요. 친절함에 감사드립니다.

Review 6-2 A

1. Choose the correct one for the blank.
(빈칸에 맞는 표현을 고르시오.)

A post office deals ______ many kinds of mails.
(우체국은 다양한 우편을 취급한다.)

a) to
b) at
c) with
d) out

정답 **c)**

2. Choose the correct one for the blank.
(빈칸에 맞는 표현을 고르시오.)

Will you pay _______cash or credit card?
(현금으로 내시겠습니까 아니면 신용카드로 내시겠습니까?)

a) for
b) by
c) before
d) after

정답 **b)**

3. **Choose the correct one for the blank.**
(빈칸에 맞는 표현을 고르시오.)

A post office distinguishes _______ ordinary mail and express mail.
(우체국은 일반 우편과 특급 우편을 구분한다.)

a) to
b) with
c) between
d) before

정답 **c)**

4. **Choose the correct one for the blank.**
(빈칸에 맞는 표현을 고르시오.)

The new mailing system of the country is ______ to none.
(그 나라의 새로운 우편 시스템은 최고이다.)

a) first
b) set
c) second
d) center

정답 **c)**

Review 6-2 B

1. **Choose the correct one for the blank.**
(빈칸에 맞는 표현을 고르시오.)

The email system has been disabled _____ technical errors.
(이메일 시스템이 기술적인 실수로 인해 고장났습니다.)

a) thanks
b) owe
c) due to
d) due

정답 c)

2. **Choose the correct one for the blank.**
(빈칸에 맞는 표현을 고르시오.)

You can _____ me an email if it is necessary.
(당신은 필요하다면 나에게 이메일을 보낼수 있습니다.)

a) sends
b) send
c) sending
d) sender

정답 b)

3. **Choose the correct one for the blank.**
(빈칸에 맞는 표현을 고르시오.)

Email comes from the expression of _______ mail.
(이메일은 전자 메일에서 온 표현이다.)

a) electrician
b) electricity
c) electronic
d) electric

정답 **c)**

4. **Choose the correct one for the blank.**
(빈칸에 맞는 표현을 고르시오.)

If you need to send a parcel, ______ it is essential.
(만약 당신이 소포를 보낼 필요가 있으면, 무게를 다는 것은 필수적이다.)

a) wait
b) weight
c) weighing
d) waiter

정답 **c)**

Scene 7 Hold on a minute

Talk 7-1

Jenson: Hello.

젠슨: 여보세요.

Amy: Hello, is Thompson there?

에이미: 여보세요, 톰슨 있어요?

Jenson: Yes, he is. Who's calling, please?

젠슨: 예, 있어요. 누구신지요?

Amy: This is Amy speaking.

에이미: 에이미입니다.

Jenson: Hi, Amy. Thompson, it's for you. It's Amy. Hold on a minute, please.

젠슨: 안녕, 에이미. 톰슨 너한테 전화 왔어. 에이미야. 잠시만 기다려.

Thompson: Hi, Amy. How was the dinner yesterday?

톰슨: 안녕, 에이미, 어제 저녁식사 어땠니?

Amy: It was fantastic. I could have a good time due to your kindness.

에이미: 끝내줬어. 너 덕에 좋은 시간 보낼수 있었지.

Thompson: I am happy to hear that. Shall we go out tonight, too?

톰슨: 기분 좋은 이야기네. 오늘 밤도 또 외출할까?

Amy: Okay. See you after work.

에이미: 좋아. 일 끝나고 보자.

Review 7-1 A

1. Choose the correct one for the blank.
(빈칸에 맞는 표현을 고르시오.)

Who is ______ please?
(전화 거시는 분 누구시지요?)

a) calling
b) call
c) calls
d) called

정답 **a)**

2. Choose the correct one for the blank.
(빈칸에 맞는 표현을 고르시오.)

_______ is Amy speaking.
(에이미입니다.)

a) This
b) That
c) These
d) Those

정답 **a)**

3. Choose the correct one for the blank.
(빈칸에 맞는 표현을 고르시오.)

Hi, Amy, _______ was the dinner, yesterday?
(안녕, 에이미, 어제 저녁 어땠어?)

a) how
b) which
c) who
d) whose

정답 **a)**

4. Choose the one which is not appropriate for the blank.
(빈칸에 알맞지 않는 표현을 고르시오.)

The dinner was ____________.

a) fantastic
b) great
c) nothing to be desired
d) nobody

정답 **d)**

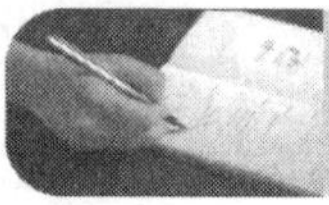

Review 7-1 B

1. **Choose the correct one for the blank.**
(빈칸에 맞는 표현을 고르시오.)

I'd like to place a ______ call to Japan.
(저는 일본으로 수신자 부담전화를 하고 싶습니다.)

a) calling
b) caller
c) collection
d) collect

정답 **d)**

2. **Choose the correct one for the blank.**
(빈칸에 맞는 표현을 고르시오.)

Please ______ me back when you are free.
(시간있을 때 나에게 전화해줘요.)

a) ring
b) calls
c) ringing
d) calling

정답 **a)**

3. **Choose the correct one for the blank.**
(빈칸에 맞는 표현을 고르시오.)

Dr. Hamilton calls you _____ the telephone.
(해밀턴 박사가 당신을 찾는 전화를 했습니다.)

a) on
b) to
c) with
d) before

정답 **a)**

4. **Choose the correct one for the blank.**
(빈칸에 맞는 표현을 고르시오.)

We have finished today's work. Let's call it a _____!
(우리는 오늘 끝났습니다. 이만 마칩시다!)

a) data
b) dance
c) date
d) day

정답 **d)**

Talk 7-2

Amy: Hello?

에이미: 여보세요?

Jenson: Good afternoon. Can I speak to Thompson at the department of accounting?

젠슨: 여보세요. 회계부서에 있는 톰슨과 통화할 수 있나요?

Amy: Hold on a moment please. Let me see whether he is in or not.

에이미: 잠깐만요. 여기 있는지 확인해 볼께요.

Amy: Hello? I am sorry to say that he is not in his room.

에이미: 여보세요? 미안하지만 그가 방에 없네요.

Jenson: Well, then can I leave a message for him?

젠슨: 그럼, 그를 위해 메시지 남길 수 있을까요?

Amy: Of course. Can you tell me who is calling?

에이미: 물론이죠. 전화하신 분이 누구신지 말씀해 주실수 있나요?

Jenson: Jenson is speaking. Please tell him to call me back. He knows my phone number.

젠슨: 젠슨이예요. 저한테 전화하라고 말씀해 주세요. 내 전화번호를 알거든요.

Amy: OK. Let me definitely carry the message.

에이미: 알았어요. 확실히 메시지를 전할께요.

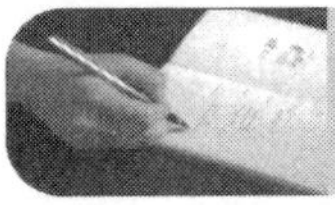

Review 7-2 A

1. **Choose the correct one for the blank.**
(빈칸에 맞는 표현을 고르시오.)

Please, _____ on a moment.
(잠깐만요.)

a) hold
b) holds
c) holding
d) holder

정답 a)

2. **Choose the correct one for the blank.**
(빈칸에 맞는 표현을 고르시오)

Let me see ______ he is in or not.
(그가 있는지 없는지 확인해 보도록 할께요.)

a) which
b) whether
c) when
d) who

정답 b)

3. **Choose the correct one for the blank.**
(빈칸에 맞는 표현을 고르시오.)

Can I leave a ______ for him.
(그를 위해 메시지를 남길 수 있을까요?)

a) mart
b) moment
c) message
d) money

정답 **c)**

4. **Choose the correct one for the blank.**
(빈칸에 맞는 표현을 고르시오.)

Please, ____ him to call me back later.
(그 사람한테 전화해달라고 말해주세요.)

a) told
b) telling
c) tell
d) teller

정답 **c)**

Review 7-2 B

1. Choose the correct one for the blank.
(빈칸에 맞는 표현을 고르시오.)

I'll _______ you with him within a minute.
(당신을 그와 곧 연결시켜 드리지요.)

a) connects
b) connection
c) connecting
d) connect

정답 **d)**

2. Choose the correct one for the blank.
(빈칸에 맞는 표현을 고르시오)

She saved her pet with the help of a 911 _____.
(그녀는 911직원의 도움으로 애완동물을 구했다.)

a) operate
b) operator
c) operates
d) operated

정답 **b)**

3. Choose the correct one for the blank.
(빈칸에 맞는 표현을 고르시오.)

When you want to _______, hang up the phone.
(전화를 끊고 싶으면, 끊으세요.)

a) disconnecter
b) disconnected
c) disconnects
d) disconnect

정답 **d)**

4. Choose the correct one for the blank.
(빈칸에 맞는 표현을 고르시오.)

If you need anything, _____ up the phone and call me.
(뭐든 필요하시다면, 수화기를 들고 전화하세요.)

a) kick
b) dick
c) pick
d) tick

정답 **c)**

Scene 8 Transportation

Talk 8-1

Jenson: How do you get to work?

젠슨: 당신은 일하러 갈 때 어떻게 가지요?

Amy: I take the subway everyday, but sometimes by bus. How about you?

에이미: 매일 지하철을 타고 갑니다. 그러나 가끔 버스 타고 갈 때가 있어요. 당신은요?

Jenson: By bus. But it is very difficult for me to use crowded buses during the rush hours.

젠슨: 버스 타고 갑니다. 출퇴근 시간에 붐비는 버스 타는 것은 힘들어요.

Amy: What time do you catch the bus?

에이미: 몇 시에 버스를 타나요?

Jenson: Almost at 8:00

젠슨: 거의 8시에요.

Amy: How long does it take you to get to work by bus?

에이미: 버스 타고 직장까지 가는데 얼마나 걸리나요?

Jenson: About half an hour.

젠슨: 약 삼십분 정도요.

Amy: Then, you will be happy with the short distance.
It takes me one hour and a half to get to work. I envy you.

에이미: 그럼, 거리가 짧아 좋으시겠네요. 저는 일하러 가는데 한시간 반이 걸립니다. 당신이 부럽네요.

Review 8-1 A

1. Choose the correct one for the blank.
(빈칸에 맞는 표현을 고르시오.)

______ do you get to work?
(당신은 어떻게 일하러 갑니까?)

a) Whose
b) Which
c) How
d) What

정답 c)

2. Choose the correct one for the blank.
(빈칸에 맞는 표현을 고르시오.)

______ do you catch the bus?
(당신은 몇시에 버스를 타시나요?)

a) What time
b) What
c) Who
d) Whose

정답 a)

3. **Choose the one which is not appropriate for the blank.**
(빈칸에 적절하지 않은 것을 고르시오)

I go to work by ________.

a) bus
b) subway
c) a taxi
d) train

정답 c)

4. **Choose the correct one for the blank.**
(빈칸에 맞는 표현을 고르시오.)

______ does it take to get to work?
(당신이 일하러 가는데 얼마나 오래 걸립니까?)

a) What
b) How
c) How long
d) Whose

정답 c)

Review 8-1 B

1. **Choose the correct one for the blank.**
(빈칸에 맞는 표현을 고르시오.)

Many people _______ to work either by bus or by subway.
(많은 사람들은 버스나 지하철로 직장까지 간다.)

a) traveling
b) traveler
c) travel
d) travels

정답 **c)**

2. **Choose the correct one for the blank.**
(빈칸에 맞는 표현을 고르시오.)

They live in a suburb and _______ to the office day after day.
(그들은 교외에서 살고 매일같이 통근한다.)

a) commutes
b) commuters
c) commute
d) commuting

정답 **c)**

3. **Choose the one which is not appropriate for the blank.**
(빈칸에 적절하지 않은 것을 고르시오)

The commuter bus is always _______.

a) busy
b) crowded
c) late
d) starter

정답 **c)**

4. **Choose the correct one for the blank.**
(빈칸에 맞는 표현을 고르시오.)

I left my house _______but I missed a bus.
(나는 일찍 집에서 떠났지만, 버스를 놓쳤다.)

a) early
b) now
c) new
d) late

정답 **a)**

Talk 8-2

Amy: Excuse me, can you tell me where I can buy a ticket?

에이미: 실례합니다. 버스표를 어디서 살 수 있는지 말씀해 주실수 있는지요?

Amy: Go straight down, and then turn right at the corner. You'll see a ticket window,

에이미: 쭈욱 내려가서, 코너에서 오른쪽으로 돌아요. 매표 창구가 보일 겁니다.

Amy: Thank you, it's very kind of you.

에이미 부인: 고맙습니다, 아주 친절하시군요.

Amy: The pleasure is mine.

에이미: 천만에요.

Amy: Good afternoon. I'd like to buy a ticket to Los Angeles.

에이미: 안녕하세요, 로스 엔젤레스로 가는 버스표를 사고 싶은데요.

Ticket Officer: What do you want? one way or round trip?

매표원: 어떤 표를 원하시는가요? 편도인가요? 왕복인가요?

Amy: Round trip, please. How much is it?

에이미: 왕복으로 주세요, 얼마죠?

Ticket Officer: That will be 80 dollars.

매표원 : 80 달러입니다.

Review 8-2 A

1. Choose the correct one for the blank.
(빈칸에 맞는 표현을 고르시오.)

It is very ______ of you, thank you.
(당신은 아주 친절하십니다, 고맙습니다.)

a) kind
b) kindness
c) happy
d) happiness

정답 **a)**

2. Choose the correct one for the blank.
(빈칸에 맞는 표현을 고르시오.)

I'd like to______ a ticket to Busan.
(나는 부산행 티켓을 사고싶습니다.)

a) buy
b) bought
c) by
d) be

정답 **a)**

3. **Choose the one which is not appropriate for the blank.**
(빈칸에 적절하지 않은 것을 고르시오)

A: Thank you for your help.
(도움에 감사드립니다.)

B: ____________________

a) The pleasure is mine
b) You're welcome
c) It is my pleasure
d) Think twice.

정답 **d)**

4. **Choose the correct one for the blank.**
(빈칸에 맞는 표현을 고르시오.)

What do you want? one way or ______ trip?
(어떤 것을 원하십니까? 편도인가요 아니면 왕복인가요?)

a) rope
b) roll
c) round
d) rotary

정답 **c)**

Review 8-2 B

1. **Choose the correct one for the blank.**
(빈칸에 맞는 표현을 고르시오.)

How long have you been _______ the wheel?
(당신은 운전하신지 얼마나 되셨습니까?)

a) between
b) behind
c) within
d) of

정답 b)

2. **Choose the correct one for the blank.**
(빈칸에 맞는 표현을 고르시오.)

We have run out of _____ along the way.
(길을 가다 차에 휘발유가 떨어졌습니다.)

a) gas
b) gases
c) gap
d) gasket

정답 a)

3. **Choose the one which is not appropriate for the blank.**
(빈칸에 적절하지 않은 것을 고르시오)

She was _______ because of a traffic jam.

a) embarrassed
b) tired
c) mad
d) happiness

정답 d)

4. **Choose the correct one for the blank.**
(빈칸에 맞는 표현을 고르시오.)

We hate _______ congestion early in the morning.
(우리는 아침 일찍 일어나는 교통 혼잡을 싫어합니다.)

a) tree
b) trout
c) trouble
d) traffic

정답 d)

Scene 9 What is your favorite season?

Talk 9-1

Jenson: Amy, what is your favorite season?

젠슨: 에이미, 어떤 계절을 가장 좋아하니?

Amy: Summer is my favorite.

에이미: 여름이 가장 좋아.

Jenson: Do you have any special reason?

젠슨: 특별한 이유가 있니?

Amy: That's because I love surfing at the beach.

에이미: 왜냐하면 해변에서 파도타기를 좋아해서 그렇지.

Jenson: Kate, what about you?

젠슨: 케이트, 너는 어때?

Kate: I like spring best. Do you know why?

케이트: 봄을 가장 좋아해. 왠지 아니?

Jenson: I want to know the reason.

젠슨: 이유를 알고 싶은데

Kate: Because I love strolling down the path of cherry blossoms.

케이트: 벚꽃 길 걷는 것을 좋아해서.

Kate: Jenson, which season do you like ?

케이트: 젠슨, 너는 어떤 계절을 좋아하니?

Jenson: I like autumn, since I love crisp air during the season.

젠슨: 나는 가을을 좋아해, 왜냐하면 그 계절의 상쾌한 공기를 좋아해서.

Review 9-1 A

1. **Choose the correct one for the blank.**
(빈칸에 맞는 표현을 고르시오.)

What is your ______ season?
(당신이 가장 좋아하는 계절은 무엇입니까?)

a) favor
b) favorite
c) fates
d) fate

정답 b)

2. **Choose the correct one for the blank.**
(빈칸에 맞는 표현을 고르시오.)

I love _______ down the path of cherry blossoms.
(나는 벚꽃 길을 거니는 것을 좋아합니다.)

a) stroller
b) strolls
c) stroll
d) strolling

정답 d)

3. Choose the one which is not appropriate for the blank.
(빈칸에 적절하지 않은 것을 고르시오)

I ________ crisp air during the season.

a) like
b) love
c) enjoy
d) fall

정답 **d)**

4. Choose the correct one for the blank.
(빈칸에 맞는 표현을 고르시오.)

I wan to know the_______ of your being late everyday.
(나는 당신이 매일 늦는 이유를 알기 원합니다.)

a) repetition
b) reasonable
c) reason
d) reaction

정답 **c)**

Review 9-1 B

1. Choose the correct one for the blank.
(빈칸에 맞는 표현을 고르시오.)

Some people look forward to ______ the seasonal change.
(일부 사람들은 계절적인 변화를 맞이하길 고대합니다.)

a) have been met
b) meeting
c) met
d) meets

정답 **b)**

2. Choose the correct one for the blank.
(빈칸에 맞는 표현을 고르시오.)

Watermelon is out of ______ this time of year.
(수박은 이맘때는 철이 아닙니다.)

a) seasonings
b) seasoning
c) seasonal
d) season

정답 **d)**

3. **Choose the one which is not appropriate for the blank.**
(빈칸에 적절하지 않은 것을 고르시오)

I ________ autumn because of my hobby.

a) like
b) love
c) enjoy
d) fall

정답 **d)**

4. **Choose the correct one for the blank.**
(빈칸에 맞는 표현을 고르시오.)

The scenery of the country varies______season to season.
(시골의 정경은 계절마다 변화한다.)

a) behind
b) for
c) from
d) at

정답 **c)**

Talk 9-2

Amy: Which season do you like best, Jenson?

에이미: 어떤 계절이 가장 좋아, 젠슨?

Jenson: I love autumn. Autumn is the best season to read books.

젠슨: 가을을 좋아해. 가을은 책읽기 가장 좋은 계절이지.

Amy: Really? do you like to read books?

에이미: 정말로? 책읽기 좋아하니?

Jenson: Yes, reading is my favorite hobby. The weather of autumn is good for reading.

젠슨: 그래, 독서는 내가 가장 좋아하는 취미야. 가을 날씨는 독서에 좋아.

Amy: Reading should be a part of your life, not hobby.

에이미: 독서는 삶의 일부가 되어야지, 취미가 아니라.

Jenson: You're definitely right. I try to read a book every day.

젠슨: 네 말이 진짜 맞아. 매일 독서하려고 노력하고 있다.

Amy: You have a good habit of reading. Reading can enrich your life.

에이미: 좋은 독서 습관을 가지고 있구나. 독서는 너의 삶을 풍요롭게 해줄 수 있어.

Jenson: That's true. Reading can change our life.

젠슨: 맞아. 독서는 우리의 삶을 바꿀 수 있어.

Review 9-2 A

1. **Choose the correct one for the blank.**
(빈칸에 맞는 표현을 고르시오.)

Which season do you like _____?
(어떤 계절을 가장 좋아하시나요?)

a) bat
b) bets
c) bests
d) best

정답 d)

2. **Choose the correct one for the blank.**
(빈칸에 맞는 표현을 고르시오.)

Autumn is the best season to ______ books.
(가을은 독서하기 가장 좋은 계절이다.)

a) read
b) reads
c) reader
d) readers

정답 a)

3. **Choose the one which is not appropriate for the blank.**
(빈칸에 적절하지 않은 것을 고르시오)

Reading can enrich ________.

a) we

b) us

c) your life

d) yourself

정답 **a)**

4. **Choose the correct one for the blank.**
(빈칸에 맞는 표현을 고르시오.)

You have a good _____ of reading.
(당신은 독서의 좋은 습관을 가지고 있습니다.)

a) herb

b) habitual

c) habitat

d) habit

정답 **d)**

Review 9-2 B

1. **Choose the correct one for the blank.**
(빈칸에 맞는 표현을 고르시오.)

________ summer I can enjoy swimming at the beach.
(여름동안에 나는 해변에서 수영을 즐길 수 있다.)

a) Which
b) Between
c) Because
d) During

정답 **d)**

2. **Choose the correct one for the blank.**
(빈칸에 맞는 표현을 고르시오.)

In Korea spring is the best season to ______ cherry blossom festival.
(한국에서는 봄이 벚꽃을 즐기기에는 최적의 계절이다.)

a) enjoy
b) enjoyable
c) enjoys
d) enjoyed

정답 **a)**

3. **Choose the one which is not appropriate for the blank.**
(빈칸에 적절하지 않은 것을 고르시오)

Some animals are nocturnal, _______ they are active at night.

a) on account of
b) because
c) as
d) since

정답 **a)**

4. **Choose the correct one for the blank.**
(빈칸에 맞는 표현을 고르시오.)

They have traveled night and _______ for a week.
(그들은 일주일간 밤낮으로 여행했다.)

a) time
b) season
c) date
d) day

정답 **d)**

Scene 10 Directions

Talk 10-1

Jenson: Excuse me. I'm looking for a city library. Is there a library in this town?

젠슨: 실례합니다. 시 도서관을 찾고 있는데요. 이 타운에 도서관이 있나요?

Thompson: Of course.

톰슨: 물론이죠.

Jenson: Can you tell me the way to the place?

젠슨: 그곳까지 가는 길을 안내해 줄수 있나요?

Thompson: No problem. Go down one block from here, and then turn to the left. You'll find it easily.

톰슨: 문제 없습니다. 여기서 한 블록 내려가시고, 그리고 왼쪽으로 가세요. 쉽게 찾으실 것입니다.

Jenson: Is it far from here?

젠슨: 여기서 머나요?

Thompson: No, it is very near from here. It's only a ten- minute walk to the library.

톰슨: 아니요, 여기서 가깝습니다. 걸어서 10분 거리입니다.

Jenson: Thank you. It's very kind of you.

젠슨: 감사합니다. 매우 친절하시네요.

Thompson: It is my pleasure.

톰슨: 천만에요.

Review 10-1 A

1. **Choose the correct one for the blank.**
(빈칸에 맞는 표현을 고르시오.)

Can you tell me the ______ to City Hall?
(시청으로 가는 길을 말씀해 주시겠습니까?)

a) party
b) moment
c) way
d) song

정답 c)

2. **Choose the correct one for the blank.**
(빈칸에 맞는 표현을 고르시오.)

Is it far ______ here?
(여기서 멉니까?)

a) by
b) from
c) to
d) at

정답 b)

3. **Choose the one which is not appropriate for the blank.**
(빈칸에 적절하지 않은 것을 고르시오)

I am _______ a city library.
(나는 시 도서관을 찾고 있는 중입니다.)

a) looking for

b) searching for

c) seeking

d) finding for

정답 d)

4. **Choose the correct one for the blank.**
(빈칸에 맞는 표현을 고르시오.)

It's only a ten- minute _____ to the library.
(도서관까지는 단지 10분이면 걸어갈 수 있는 거리입니다.)

a) walked

b) walks

c) walk

d) walker

정답 c)

Review 10-1 B

1. **Choose the correct one for the blank.**
(빈칸에 맞는 표현을 고르시오.)

She ______ to Switzerland one year ago.
(그녀는 1년 전에 스위스로 갔습니다.)

a) gone
b) goes
c) went
d) go

정답 **c)**

2. **Choose the correct one for the blank.**
(빈칸에 맞는 표현을 고르시오.)

His office is _____ the second floor of this building.
(그의 사무실은 이 빌딩의 2층에 있습니다.)

a) by
b) off
c) on
d) at

정답 **c)**

3. **Choose the one which is not appropriate for the blank.**
(빈칸에 적절하지 않은 것을 고르시오)

Mt. Halla is a ________ for foreign tourists.

a) good place
b) must
c) tourist spot
d) can

정답 **d)**

4. **Choose the correct one for the blank.**
(빈칸에 맞는 표현을 고르시오.)

The college is located _____ front of a small hill.
(그 대학은 작은 언덕 앞에 위치한다.)

a) from
b) at
c) in
d) with

정답 **c)**

Talk 10-2

Jenson: Is this the right way to the Seoul station?
젠슨: 이 길이 서울 역으로 가는 맞는 길인가요?

Thompson: Yes, it is.
톰슨: 맞아요.

Jenson: Can I go there by bus?
젠슨: 거기까지 버스 타고 갈 수 있나요?

Thompson: Yes, you can. It will take 20 minutes from here to the place by bus.
톰슨: 예, 그럼요. 여기서 그곳까지 버스로 20분 걸립니다.

Jenson: What number of the bus should I take?
젠슨: 몇 번 버스를 타야 합니까?

Thompson: You should take the bus of the blue line. The bus number is 122.
톰슨: 파란 라인 버스를 타셔야 합니다. 122번 버스를 타셔야 합니다.

Jenson: Thank you very much.
젠슨: 대단히 고맙습니다.

Thompson: No, problem. My pleasure.
톰슨: 천만에요.

Review 10-2 A

1. **Choose the correct one for the blank.**
(빈칸에 맞는 표현을 고르시오.)

Is this the ____ to Itaewon?
(이태원으로 가는 길인가요?)

a) man
b) shop
c) way
d) soap

정답 **c)**

2. **Choose the correct one for the blank.**
(빈칸에 맞는 표현을 고르시오.)

Can I go there ___ train?
(제가 기차로 거기 갈수 있나요?)

a) over
b) beyond
c) with
d) by

정답 **d)**

3. **Choose the one which is not appropriate for the blank.**
(빈칸에 적절하지 않은 것을 고르시오)

You should take the bus of _______.

a) blue line

b) red line

c) No. 122.

d) rules

정답 d)

4. **Choose the correct one for the blank.**
(빈칸에 맞는 표현을 고르시오.)

What kind of bus should I ______ ?
(어떤 종류의 버스를 제가 타야 합니까?)

a) taken

b) takes

c) take

d) taking

정답 c)

Review 10-2 B

1. Choose the correct one for the blank.
(빈칸에 맞는 표현을 고르시오.)

The bus terminal is _____ five minutes' walk from my house.
(버스 터미널은 나의 집에서 5분 걸음 이내에 있다.)

a) what
b) which
c) with
d) within

정답 d)

2. Choose the correct one for the blank.
(빈칸에 맞는 표현을 고르시오.)

Is there a bus station _______?
(근처에 버스 역 있나요?)

a) most
b) mostly
c) nearly
d) nearby

정답 d)

3. **Choose the one which is not appropriate for the blank.**
(빈칸에 적절하지 않은 것을 고르시오)

Seoul is ________ the regular bus service.

a) well equipped with
b) famous for
c) a good city for us to use
d) looked for

정답 **d)**

4. **Choose the correct one for the blank.**
(빈칸에 맞는 표현을 고르시오.)

Do not _______ a U-turn in the middle of the road without signs.
(신호없이는 도로중간에서 유턴하지 마세요.)

a) make
b) making
c) take
d) taking

정답 **a)**

Scene 11 Reservation

Talk 11-1

Staff: Good afternoon, what can I do for you?
직원: 안녕하세요, 무엇을 도와 드릴까요?

Thompson: Good afternoon. Isn't Korean Air reservation department? I'd like to make an airline ticket reservation.
톰슨: 안녕하세요. 대한항공 예약부인가요? 항공편 티켓 예약하고 싶은데요.

Staff: Yes, this is reservation department, sir. Where are you going?
직원: 대한항공 예약부 맞습니다, 선생님. 어디로 가실 예정인가요?

Thompson: To Los Angeles
톰슨: 뉴욕으로 갈 건데요.

Staff: When are you leaving?
직원: 언제 떠나실 건가요?

Thompson: Upcoming Saturday
톰슨: 다가오는 토요일에요

Staff: What time are you going to leave?
직원: 몇 시에 출발 하실 건가요?

Thompson: At 9:30 in the morning.
톰슨: 아침 9시 반에요.

Staff: Good. your airline ticket has been booked now.
직원: 좋습니다. 귀하의 항공편이 지금 예약되었습니다.

Thompson: I appreciate your kindness and help.
톰슨: 친절과 도움에 감사합니다.

Staff: You're welcome. Have a nice day.
직원: 천만에요. 좋은 하루 보내십시오.

Review 11-1 A

1. **Choose the correct one for the blank.**
(빈칸에 맞는 표현을 고르시오.)

_______ time are you going to leave?
(당신은 몇 시에 떠나실겁니까?)

a) What
b) When
c) Whose
d) Who

정답 **a)**

2. **Choose the correct one for the blank.**
(빈칸에 맞는 표현을 고르시오.)

I _________ your kindness and help.
(당신의 친절함에 감사드려요.)

a) appreciate
b) appreciates
c) appreciating
d) appreciation

정답 **a)**

3. **Choose the one which is not appropriate for the blank.**
(빈칸에 적절하지 않은 것을 고르시오)

When are you _______ ?

a) leaving
b) going
c) arriving
d) seeing

정답 **d)**

4. **Choose the correct one for the blank.**
(빈칸에 맞는 표현을 고르시오.)

Your airline ticket has been _______ now.
(당신의 비행기 티켓이 지금 예약되었습니다.)

a) booking
b) books
c) book
d) booked

정답 **d)**

Review 11-1 B

1. Choose the correct one for the blank.
(빈칸에 맞는 표현을 고르시오.)

The arrival of the flight has been ______ due to bad weather.

(비행도착이 나쁜 날씨로 인해 연기되었다.)

a) delayed

b) driven

c) taken

d) brought

정답 a)

2. Choose the correct one for the blank.
(빈칸에 맞는 표현을 고르시오.)

How many pieces of _______ are you carrying?
(얼마나 많은 짐을 나르고 있습니까?)

a) baggage

b) baggages

c) luggages

d) furnitures

정답 a)

3. **Choose the one which is not appropriate for the blank.**
(빈칸에 적절하지 않은 것을 고르시오)

Where can I _____ a cheap airline ticket on the internet?

a) buy
b) purchase
c) get
d) attend

정답 **d)**

4. **Choose the correct one for the blank.**
(빈칸에 맞는 표현을 고르시오.)

Where is the final ________ of your trip?
(당신 여행의 최종 목적지가 어디입니까?)

a) deletion
b) delight
c) destiny
d) destination

정답 **d)**

Talk 11-2

Staff: Good morning, Korean Air. How may I help you?

직원 : 안녕하세요. 대한항공입니다. 어떻게 도와드릴까요?

Amy: Good morning, let me reserve a flight ticket to New Mexico from Incheon Airport.

에이미: 인천공항에서 뉴 멕시코행 항공편을 예약하고 싶은데요.

Staff: When is your departure date?

직원 : 출발 날짜가 언제이신가요?

Amy: Next Thursday, March 22nd. Can I leave as early as possible on that day?

에이미: 다음주 목요일, 22일이에요. 그날 가능한한 일찍 출발할 수 있나요?

Staff: You can leave at 8:30 at the earliest in the morning,

직원 : 빨라야 아침 8시 30분입니다.

Amy: Not bad. let me take it.

에이미: 괜찮은데요. 그것으로 하죠.

Staff: Okay. You have a reservation to New Mexico from Incheon on Thursday, March 22nd at 8;30. Is it one way or round trip?

직원 : 알았습니다. 다음주 목요일 8시 30분 인천 발 뉴멕시코 도착행 비행편이 예약되었습니다. 편도입니까, 왕복입니까?

Amy: One way, please

에이미: 편도 부탁드립니다.

Staff: Okay, your one way ticket has been reserved. Please check in at least one and half an hour before departure time. Thank you.

직원 : 좋습니다, 편도 티켓이 예약되었습니다. 출발시간 한시간 반 전에 수속을 밟으십시오.

감사합니다.

Review 11-2 A

1. Choose the correct one for the blank.
(빈칸에 맞는 표현을 고르시오.)

How _____ I help you?
(어떻게 도와드릴까요?)

a) does
b) are
c) may
d) dare

정답 **c)**

2. Choose the correct one for the blank.
(빈칸에 맞는 표현을 고르시오.)

You can leave at 8:30 at the _______ in the morning.
(당신은 아침에 가장 빨리 8:30분에 떠날 수 있습니다.)

a) early
b) earliest
c) yearly
d) year

정답 **b)**

3. **Choose the one which is not appropriate for the blank.**
(빈칸에 적절하지 않은 것을 고르시오)

Not bad. let me ______ it.

a) choose
b) have
c) walk
d) take

정답 c)

4. **Choose the correct one for the blank.**
(빈칸에 맞는 표현을 고르시오.)

You have a________ of flight ticket to New Mexico.
(당신은 뉴멕시코 비행기 티켓 예약이 되어 있습니다.)

a) reserving
b) reserves
c) reservation
d) reserve

정답 c)

Review 11-2 B

1. **Choose the correct one for the blank.**

(빈칸에 맞는 표현을 고르시오.)

The airplane is _______ off from Incheon airport.

(비행기는 인천공항을 이륙하는 중입니다.)

a) takes

b) take

c) taking

d) taken

정답 **c)**

2. **Choose the correct one for the blank.**

(빈칸에 맞는 표현을 고르시오.)

Do you have anything to _________?

(당신은 신고하실 것 있습니까?)

a) declares

b) declare

c) declaring

d) declaration

정답 **b)**

3. **Choose the one which is not appropriate for the blank.**
(빈칸에 적절하지 않은 것을 고르시오)

The airplane ___________ Gimpo airport.

a) is landing on
b) takes off from
c) arrives at
d) is going

정답 **d)**

4. **Choose the correct one for the blank.**
(빈칸에 맞는 표현을 고르시오.)

You need to _____ out the customs declaration form.
(당신은 세관 신고서를 작성할 필요가 있습니다.)

a) pull
b) pill
c) fill
d) full

정답 **c)**

Scene 12 Disease

Talk 12-1

Jenson: Hi, Amy. It's time for lunch. What do you want to have for lunch?

젠슨: 안녕. 에이미. 점심시간이다. 점심 뭐 먹을래?

Amy: Thank you for your offer, but I am suffering from diarrhea.

에이미: 미안해. 점심 먹으러 갈 수 없어. 저녁은 어때?

Jenson: That's too bad. When were you feeling bad ?

젠슨: 안되었구나. 언제 아팠니?

Amy: Since last night I've been so sick and even vomitting.

에이미: 어제 밤부터 아주 아팠고 토하기까지 했어.

Jenson: And then, you'd better leave work early and see a doctor.

젠슨: 그러면, 일찍 퇴근해서 의사 진찰 받는게 좋겠다.

Amy: You're right. Thank you for your consideration.

에이미: 네말이 맞아. 생각해 줘서 고마워.

Jenson: Don't mention it. Let me give you a ride to a hospital if you need.

젠슨: 천만에. 필요하면 병원에 태워다 줄게,

Amy: How sweet you are. You look like an angel.

에이미: 멋지다. 너 천사처럼 보여.

Review 12-1 A

1. **Choose the correct one for the blank.**
(빈칸에 맞는 표현을 고르시오.)

What do you want to have_____ lunch?
(당신은 점심으로 무엇을 드시길 원하십니까?)

a) behind
b) in
c) for
d) to

정답 **c)**

2. **Choose the correct one for the blank.**
(빈칸에 맞는 표현을 고르시오.)

I am _______ from diarrhea.
(나는 설사로 고생하는 중이다.)

a) surf
b) surfing
c) suffer
d) suffering

정답 **d)**

3. Choose the one which is not appropriate for the blank.
(빈칸에 적절하지 않은 것을 고르시오)

I was so ______ and even vomitting.

a) sick
b) tired
c) exhausted
d) happy

정답 **d)**

4. Choose the correct one for the blank.
(빈칸에 맞는 표현을 고르시오.)

Let me give you a _____ to a hospital.
(병원까지 태워다 드리겠습니다.)

a) walk
b) walks
c) ride
d) rides

정답 **c)**

Review 12-1 B

1. Choose the correct one for the blank.
(빈칸에 맞는 표현을 고르시오.)

Jenson called in ______ early in the morning.
(젠슨은 아침 일찍 아파서 못온다고 전화했다.)

a) illness
b) ill
c) sick
d) sickness

정답 **c)**

2. Choose the correct one for the blank.
(빈칸에 맞는 표현을 고르시오.)

My insurance policy ________ even surgery.
(내 보험 약관은 수술까지 보장한다.)

a) have covered
b) cover
c) covering
d) covers

정답 **d)**

3. Choose the one which is not appropriate for the blank.
(빈칸에 적절하지 않은 것을 고르시오)

_______ can help you recover from a number of illnesses.

a) Some drug
b) Some medicine
c) Antibiotics
d) Ailment

정답 **d)**

4. Choose the correct one for the blank.
(빈칸에 맞는 표현을 고르시오.)

He _______ a severe cold last night.
(그는 지난밤에 심한 감기에 걸렸다.)

a) caught
b) made
c) exhausted
d) took

정답 **a)**

Talk 12-2

Jenson: Amy, have you been feeling bad until now?

젠슨: 에이미, 지금까지 아프니?

Amy: Yes, I have been suffering from backache, and arthritis of my right arm.

에이미: 네, 허리통증과 오픈 팔 관절염으로 인해 고생하고 있어요.

Jenson: Did you take any pills to cure your symptoms?

젠슨: 증세를 치료하기 위해 약 먹었니?

Amy: I'd love to. But I couldn't see a doctor due to my busy schedule.

에이미: 가고 싶었죠. 그런데 바쁜 스케줄 때문에 진찰을 못받았어.

Jenson: Let me take over your work, and you can leave early.

젠슨: 내가 너의 일을 맡을께. 그러면 너는 일찍 갈수 있지.

Amy: Thank you for your kindness, but I am afraid of my stubborn boss.

에이미: 친절함에 고맙지만, 완고한 사장님이 두렵네.

Jenson: Don't worry about it. Our boss is out of town now for our clients.
But he'll understand it.

젠슨: 걱정마. 사장님이 고객 때문에 출타중이셔. 하지만 이해하실거야.

Amy: All right, let's make a reservation call to the hospital first.

에이미: 좋아, 병원에 예약 전화 먼저하자.

Jenson: It sounds like a good idea.

젠슨: 좋은 생각이야.

Review 12-2 A

1. **Choose the correct one for the blank.**
(빈칸에 맞는 표현을 고르시오.)

Did you _____ any pills to cure your symptoms?
(당신은 증상을 치료하기 위해 약을 복용하나요?)

a) takes
b) take
c) taken
d) took

정답 **b)**

2. **Choose the correct one for the blank.**
(빈칸에 맞는 표현을 고르시오.)

Let me take ______ your work,
(당신의 일을 제가 넘겨 받겠습니다.)

a) by
b) beyond
c) with
d) over

정답 **d)**

3. **Choose the one which is not appropriate for the blank.**
(빈칸에 적절하지 않은 것을 고르시오)

Don't ______________ it

a) worry about
b) mention
c) touch
d) look

정답 **d)**

4. **Choose the correct one for the blank.**
(빈칸에 맞는 표현을 고르시오.)

I am afraid ___ my supervisor when he is angry.
(나의 상사가 화날 때 그분이 두렵다.)

a) after
b) with
c) of
d) on

정답 **c)**

Review 12-2 B

1. Choose the correct one for the blank.
(빈칸에 맞는 표현을 고르시오.)

She looks very tired, and she'd better ______ a rest.
(그녀는 피곤해 보인다. 그녀는 휴식을 취하는 것이 좋겠다.)

a) takes
b) take
c) taken
d) took

정답 **b)**

2. Choose the correct one for the blank.
(빈칸에 맞는 표현을 고르시오.)

She is always careful ______ taking medicine.
(그녀는 항상 약 복용하는 것에 주의한다.)

a) by
b) off
c) with
d) of

정답 **d)**

3. **Choose the one which is not appropriate for the blank.**
(빈칸에 적절하지 않은 것을 고르시오)

Dr. Cruz is a/an ___________ physician.

a) skilled
b) experienced
c) good
d) newly

정답 **d)**

4. **Choose the correct one for the blank.**
(빈칸에 맞는 표현을 고르시오.)

The regular______ checkup is necessary for your health.
(정기 검진은 당신의 건강을 위해 필요하다.)

a) medicinal
b) medic
c) medical
d) medicine

정답 **c)**

Scene 13 Travel

Talk 13-1

Jenson: I'm going to travel Canada this weekend. Have you ever traveled Canada?

젠슨: 이번 주말에 캐나다에 갈 계획이야. 캐나다에 가 본 적이 있니?

Amy: No, how many countries have you visited?

에이미: 아니, 얼마나 많은 나라를 가 보았니?

Jenson: Two countries until now. I've traveled U.S.A and New Zealand.

젠슨: 지금까지 두군데 가 봤어. 미국하고 뉴질랜드를 여행했지.

Amy: I envy you. Will you travel more countries in the near future?

에이미: 부럽다. 가까운 장래에 더 많은 나라를 여행할거니?

Jenson: Absolutely. I want to travel as many countries as possible.

젠슨: 아니. 일년 반 정도 더 여기에 있을 거야.

Amy: Wow, you enjoy your life well.

에이미: 와. 너는 너의 인생을 잘 즐기는 구나.

Jenson: I am just trying to live my life as I want to.

젠슨: 나는 내가 하고싶은대로 살려고 하는거야.

Amy: You are the real master of your life. Have a good trip to Canada during your leave.

에이미: 너는 네 인생의 진짜 주인이구나. 휴가 기간동안에 캐나다 잘 갔다와.

Review 13-1 A

1. **Choose the correct one for the blank.**
(빈칸에 맞는 표현을 고르시오.)

Have you ________ traveled Canada?
(당신은 캐나다 여행해 본적 있나요?)

a) event
b) eve
c) every
d) ever

정답 **d)**

2. **Choose the correct one for the blank.**
(빈칸에 맞는 표현을 고르시오.)

I've ________ Korea and China in my life.
(나는 내인생에서 한국과 중국을 여행했다.)

a) travel
b) traveled
c) travels
d) travelling

정답 **b)**

3. **Choose the one which is not appropriate for the blank.**
(빈칸에 적절하지 않은 것을 고르시오)

I am just trying to ______ my life well.

a) enjoy
b) look
c) live
d) lead

정답 **b)**

4. **Choose the correct one for the blank.**
(빈칸에 맞는 표현을 고르시오.)

Have a good _______ to Canada during your leave.
(당신의 휴가동안에 캐나다로 좋은 여행 하십시오.)

a) trip
b) tripping
c) traveler
d) trouble

정답 **a)**

Review 13-1 B

1. Choose the correct one for the blank.
(빈칸에 맞는 표현을 고르시오.)

Ms. McCarthy wants to travel all ______ the world.
(미스 맥카시는 전세계를 여행하기를 원한다.)

a) on
b) at
c) to
d) over

정답 **d)**

2. Choose the correct one for the blank.
(빈칸에 맞는 표현을 고르시오.)

A tourist has stopped to ______ a rest under a tree.
(여행가는 나무아래에서 쉬기 위해 멈췄다.)

a) have
b) do
c) travel
d) move

정답 **a)**

3. Choose the correct one for the blank.
(빈칸에 맞는 표현을 고르시오.)

He ______ for a business trip two days ago.
(그는 이틀 전에 출장을 떠났다.)

a) took
b) left
c) live
d) led

정답 b)

4. Choose the correct one for the blank.
(빈칸에 맞는 표현을 고르시오.)

I was on a ocean ______ when you called me.
(나는 당신이 전화했을 때 바다 여행중이었다.)

a) voyage
b) tripping
c) buoy
d) poll

정답 a)

Talk 13-2

Jenson: Have you ever been to Tokyo?

젠슨: 도쿄에 가본적 있나요?

Thompson: Yes, I've been there twice.

톰슨: 네, 두 번이요.

Jenson: How was the trip to Tokyo?

젠슨: 도쿄 여행 어땠나요?

Thompson: It was fantastic. I especially enjoyed sushi and raw fish.

톰슨: 좋았어요. 특별히 스시와 회를 즐겼습니다.

Jenson: Would you recommend a tourist spot in Tokyo? I go to Tokyo for my leave with my family.

젠슨: 도쿄 관광명소를 추천해주실래요? 휴가를 위해 가족들과 도쿄 갑니다.

Thompson: Of course. I strongly recommend Hakone for your leave.

톰슨: 물론이죠. 나는 하코네를 강력히 추천합니다.

Jenson: Why do you recommend Hakone?

젠슨: 왜 하코네를 추천하시죠?

Thompson: Hakone is famous for hot spring and a serene forest. It is not that far from the heart of Tokyo.

톰슨: 하코네는 온천과 조용한 숲으로 유명하죠. 도쿄 중심가에서 그리 멀지 않아요.

Jenson: It sounds great. Thank you for your recommendation.

젠슨: 좋습니다. 추천해주셔서 감사합니다.

Thompson: Your welcome. Hopefully you enjoy your trip to Tokyo,

톰슨: 천만에요. 바라건대 도쿄여행 즐기시길 빕니다.

Review 13-2 A

1. **Choose the correct one for the blank.**
(빈칸에 맞는 표현을 고르시오.)

Have you ever _______ to Tokyo?
(당신은 도쿄 가보신적 있나요?)

a) be
b) is
c) been
d) are

정답 **c)**

2. **Choose the correct one for the blank.**
(빈칸에 맞는 표현을 고르시오.)

Would you _______ a tourist spot in Tokyo?
(도쿄 관광명소를 추천해 주시겠습니까?)

a) recommend
b) recommending
c) recommendable
d) recommends

정답 **a)**

3. **Choose the one which is not appropriate for the blank.**
(빈칸에 적절하지 않은 것을 고르시오)

A travel ______ booked our hotel reservation.

a) agent
b) agency
c) conductor
d) tutor

정답 **d)**

4. **Choose the correct one for the blank.**
(빈칸에 맞는 표현을 고르시오.)

The concierge can help you ____ your needs during your stay.
(관리인은 당신이 머무는 동안에 당신의 요구한 것을 도와줄 것이다.)

a) at
b) between
c) to
d) with

정답 **d)**

Review 13-2 B

1. **Choose the correct one for the blank.**
(빈칸에 맞는 표현을 고르시오.)

The renovated amusement park has become a tourist ______.
(리모델링한 놀이 공원은 관광명소가 되었다.)

a) attractive
b) attracting
c) attraction
d) attracts

정답 **c)**

2. **Choose the correct one for the blank.**
(빈칸에 맞는 표현을 고르시오.)

She went to a travel ______ to buy a cheap air ticket.
(그녀는 값싼 비행기 표를 사기위해 여행사로 갔다.)

a) agenda
b) aging
c) age
d) agency

정답 **d)**

3. **Choose the one which is not appropriate for the blank.**
(빈칸에 적절하지 않은 것을 고르시오)

Hakone ____ famous for hot spring and a serene forest.

a) has been
b) was
c) is
d) does

정답 **d)**

4. **Choose the correct one for the blank.**
(빈칸에 맞는 표현을 고르시오.)

Hopefully you ________ your trip to Tokyo.
(바란건데 도쿄여행 즐기시길 빕니다.)

a) enjoys
b) enjoying
c) enjoy
d) enjoyable

정답 **c)**

Scene 14 Job Interview

Talk 14-1

Jenson: Good morning. I came here for my job interview.
젠슨: 안녕하세요. 취업 면접을 위해 여기 왔습니다.

Secretary: Wait a moment, please. Can you tell me your name?
비서: 잠깐만요. 성함좀 말씀해 주시겠어요?

Jenson: I'm Jenson.
젠슨: 젠슨입니다.

Secretary: What's your sur name?
비서: 성이 무엇입니까?

Jenson: Cruz
젠슨: 쿠르즈입니다.

Secretary: How do you spell it?
비서: 철자가 어떻게 됩니까?

Jenson: C-R-U-Z.
젠슨: 씨 알 유 젵

Secretary: Great. Please come in for your interview.
비서: 좋습니다. 인터뷰를 위해 안으로 들어오세요.

Interviewer: Please introduce yourself to us.
면접관: 우리에게 자신을 소개해 보세요.

Jenson: Good morning, sirs. My name is Jenson Cruz. I am 21 years old. I graduated from Chicago University. I majored in international finance at the department of Economy of the school. And I acquired the certificate of accountant in New York.

젠슨: 안녕하십니까. 제 이름은 젠슨 쿠르즈입니다. 21세이고 시카고 대학을 졸업했습니다. 시카고 대학 경제학과에서 국제 금융을 전공했습니다. 그리고 뉴욕 회계사 자격증을 취득했습니다.

Interviewer: Okay, why did you apply for our company?

면접관: 좋아요, 왜 우리 회사에 지원했나요?

Jenson: Simpson inc. is leading the field of corporate finance in the world. I want to work as an accountant in that field.

젠슨: 심슨회사는 세계에서 기업 금융분야를 이끌고 있습니다. 그 분야에서 회계사로 일하고 싶습니다.

Interviewer: Okay, You are one of the qualified applicants. Good luck to you.

면접관: 좋아요. 당신은 자격 있는 지원자중에 한분이시네요. 행운을 빕니다.

Review 14-1 A

1. **Choose the correct one for the blank.**
(빈칸에 맞는 표현을 고르시오.)

I came here______ my job interview.
(나는 취업면접을 위해 여기에 왔습니다.)

a) for
b) with
c) on
d) at

정답 **a)**

2. **Choose the correct one for the blank.**
(빈칸에 맞는 표현을 고르시오.)

It ___ leading the field of international finance.
(그곳은 국제 금융분야를 이끌고 있습니다.)

a) were
b) is
c) has
d) have

정답 **b)**

3. **Choose the one which is not appropriate for the blank.**
(빈칸에 적절하지 않은 것을 고르시오)

You are one of the qualified ________.

a) personnel
b) students
c) applicants
d) person

정답 **d)**

4. **Choose the correct one for the blank.**
(빈칸에 맞는 표현을 고르시오.)

Why did you _______ for our company?
(왜 당신은 우리 회사에 지원하셨나요?)

a) applicant
b) apply
c) application
d) applied

정답 **b)**

Review 14-1 B

1. **Choose the correct one for the blank.**
(빈칸에 맞는 표현을 고르시오.)

We'll _______ your application.
(우리는 당신의 응시원서를 검토할 것입니다.)

a) looks
b) look
c) looking
d) look over

정답 **d)**

2. **Choose the correct one for the blank.**
(빈칸에 맞는 표현을 고르시오.)

What are job _________ of your company?
(우리 회사의 취업 요구사항이 무엇입니까?)

a) require
b) requirements
c) requires
d) requiring

정답 **b)**

3 **Choose the correct one for the blank.**
(빈칸에 맞는 표현을 고르시오.)

The interviewer works for the department of _______.
(그 면접관은 인사부에서 일한다.)

a) personnel

b) students

c) applicants

d) person

정답 **a)**

4. **Choose the correct one for the blank.**
(빈칸에 맞는 표현을 고르시오.)

Are you a/an ______ for our company?
(당신은 우리 회사의 지원자입니까?

a) applicant

b) apply

c) application

d) applied

정답 **a)**

Talk 14-2

Interviewer: Good morning, please introduce yourself, Mr. Jenson Cruz.

면접관: 안녕하세요, 자신을 소개해 보세요, 젠슨 크루즈씨.

Jenson: Thank you very much for the opportunity for the job interview.

I am Jenson Cruz. I am a student at the department of business adminstration of Hankuk College.

젠슨: 취업 인터뷰 기회에 대해서 아주 감사드립니다. 저는 젠슨 쿠르즈입니다. 한국대학 경영학과의 학생입니다.

Interviewer: Do you have any experience of part- time job?

면접관: 아르바이트 해본 경험 있나요?

Jenson: Yes, I do. I worked part-time job for my tuition and living expenses.

젠슨: 네, 그렇습니다. 저는 수업료와 생활비를 위해 아르바이트를 했습니다.

Interviewer: What kind of part-time job did you have?

면접관: 어떤 종류의 아르바이트였나요?

Jenson: I worked as an English interpreter for the foreign investors to Korean companies.

젠슨: 한국 기업의 해외 투자자들을 위한 영어 통역사로 일했습니다.

Interviewer: How was it?

면접관: 어땠나요?

Jenson: It was well paid. I loved it. But, frankly speaking, I want to have a more stable job like your company.

젠슨: 돈벌이는 되었습니다. 좋아했구요. 하지만 솔직히 말하면 귀사와 같은 곳에서 더 안정적인 일을 갖고 싶습니다.

Interviewer: You look very honest. Thank you for the interview. Good luck to you.

면접관: 솔직해 보이시네요. 인터뷰 감사합니다. 행운을 빌어요.

Review 14-2 A

1. **Choose the correct one for the blank.**
(빈칸에 맞는 표현을 고르시오.)

Thank you very much for the ________.

a) opportunity
b) stable
c) paid
d) invest

정답 **a)**

2. **Choose the correct one for the blank.**
(빈칸에 맞는 표현을 고르시오.)

I worked _____ an English interpreter.

a) on
b) at
c) to
d) as

정답 **d)**

3. **Choose the one which is not appropriate for the blank.**
(빈칸에 적절하지 않은 것을 고르시오)

__________, I want to have a good job from your company.

a) Frankly speaking
b) To be honest
c) Honestly
d) Honest

정답 **d)**

4. **Choose the correct one for the blank.**
(빈칸에 맞는 표현을 고르시오.)

Jane wants to have a more_______ job, due to her sick baby.
(자넷은 그녀의 아픈 아기 때문에 더 안정적인 일을 가지고자 한다.)

a) street
b) star
c) stable
d) start

정답 **c)**

Review 14–2 B

1. **Choose the correct one for the blank.**
(빈칸에 맞는 표현을 고르시오.)

The biggest problem for ________ is speech.
(면접자들의 가장 큰 문제는 말이다.)

a) interviewees
b) internal
c) intra
d) intrigue

정답 **a)**

2. **Choose the correct one for the blank.**
(빈칸에 맞는 표현을 고르시오.)

The interviewers will interview you in _______.
(면접관들은 당신을 심층 면접할 것입니다.)

a) dear
b) deer
c) deep
d) depth

정답 **d)**

3. **Choose the correct one for the blank.**
(빈칸에 맞는 표현을 고르시오.)

He was nervous around the _____ before a job interview.
(그는 취업 면접 전에 24시간 긴장했다.)

a) click
b) clock
c) cloth
d) clear

정답 **b)**

4. **Choose the correct one for the blank.**
(빈칸에 맞는 표현을 고르시오.)

The managing director is my ________.
(전무이사는 나의 상사이다.)

a) steep
b) supervisor
c) super
d) start

정답 **b)**

Scene 15 Weather

Talk 15-1

Jenson: It's a beautiful day, isn't it?

젠슨: 날씨가 참 좋네요, 그렇죠?

Amy: Yes. I like the clear weather.

에이미: 그래요. 저는 맑은 날이 좋아요.

Jenson: How was the weather yesterday? I came home from my business trip yesterday.

젠슨: 어제 날씨는 어땠어요? 저는 출장에서 어제 집에 돌아왔거든요.

Amy: It rained cats and dogs. The torrential rain brought a disaster to the farmers.

에이미: 비가 억수같이 왔었어요. 폭우로 인해 농부들에게 재앙이 닥쳤지요.

Jenson: That's too bad. I am afraid that farmers are suffering from the disastrous weather.

젠슨: 안되었네요. 농부들이 재앙스러운 날씨로 인해 고생할까봐 두려워요.

Amy: A weather forecaster says it is expected to rain heavily again tomorrow.

에이미: 일기예보관이 내일 또 비가 많이 온다네요.

Jenson: I am sorry to hear that. I would rather cancel going camping to Gangwon Province with my family.

젠슨: 유감이군요. 가족하고 강원도로 캠핑가는 것을 차라리 취소해야겠어요.

Amy: You are right. You should be careful with the harsh weather these days.

에이미: 맞아요. 요즘 거친 날씨에 주의하셔야지요.

Review 15-1 A

1. Choose the correct one for the blank.
(빈칸에 맞는 표현을 고르시오.)

I came home _______ my business trip.
(나는 출장갔다 집으로 돌아왔다.)

a) to
b) from
c) at
d) on

정답 **b)**

2. Choose the correct one for the blank.
(빈칸에 맞는 표현을 고르시오.)

I am afraid ____ farmers are suffering from bad weather.
(나는 농부들이 나쁜 날씨로 고생할까봐 두렵다.)

a) by
b) that
c) into
d) at

정답 **b)**

3. **Choose the one which is not appropriate for the blank.**
(빈칸에 적절하지 않은 것을 고르시오)

I am ______ to hear that.

a) sorry
b) happy
c) pleased
d) wonderful

정답 **d)**

4. **Choose the correct one for the blank.**
(빈칸에 맞는 표현을 고르시오.)

You should _____ careful with harsh weather.
(당신은 거친 날씨에 주의를 기울여야 한다.)

a) are
b) be
c) is
d) were

정답 **b)**

Review 15-1 B

1. **Choose the correct one for the blank.**
(빈칸에 맞는 표현을 고르시오.)

A weather forecaster says it is expected to rain ______.
(일기 예보관은 비가 심하게 올것이라고 말합니다.)

a) heaviness
b) heavily
c) heat
d) heating

정답 **b)**

2. **Choose the correct one for the blank.**
(빈칸에 맞는 표현을 고르시오.)

A meteorologist is __________ a hurricane.
(기상학자는 허리케인을 예상하고 있습니다.)

a) expect
b) expects
c) expecting
d) expecter

정답 **c)**

3. **Choose the one which is not appropriate for the blank.**
(빈칸에 적절하지 않은 것을 고르시오)

A blizzard is a long and ________ snow storm.

a) heavy
b) intense
c) dreadful
d) warm

정답 d)

4. **Choose the correct one for the blank.**
(빈칸에 맞는 표현을 고르시오.)

The typhoon _______ a serious damage throughout the country.
(태풍은 전국에 걸쳐 심각한 손상을 초래했다.)

a) causeful
b) causing
c) cause
d) caused

정답 d)

Talk 15-2

Jenson: The weather forecast has been unreliable these days.

젠슨: 날씨가 요즘 믿을수가 없어요.

Amy: You are right. It is because of changeable weather.

에이미: 그래요. 변덕스러운 날씨 때문에 그렇죠.

Jenson: Why is the weather so changeable and unpredictable?

젠슨: 왜 날씨가 변화가 심하고 예측불가능 한거죠?

Amy: Climate has been changed dramatically these days. Additionally climate change is a serious problem.

에이미: 기후가 요즘 급격하게 바뀌었구요. 게다가 기후 변화는 심각한 문제입니다.

Jenson: I know your point. But I am asking you why it is so changeable.

젠슨: 말하는 것 압니다. 하지만 왜 변화가 심한지 묻고 있는 겁니다.

Amy: That is because of El Nino and La Nina. They are affecting the weather temperatures around the world.

에이미: 엘니뇨와 라니냐 때문이죠. 그것들이 전세계 기온에 영향을 주고 있어요.

Jenson: I see. I heard that the butterfly effect has been originated from the weather.

젠슨: 알겠어요. 나비효과가 날씨로부터 기원했다고 들었어요.

Amy: You are right. The butterfly effect theory was created by an American meteorologist, Edward Norton Lorenz in 1961.

에이미: 맞아요. 나비 효과 이론은 미국 기상학자인 에드워드 로렌즈에의해 1961년 만들어졌지요.

Jenson: Wow, you must be a Mr. Know-It-All.

젠슨: 대단하네요. 당신은 만물박사임에 틀림없습니다.

Review 15-2 A

1. **Choose the correct one for the blank.**
(빈칸에 맞는 표현을 고르시오.)
The weather forecast has _______ unreliable these days.
(일기 예보는 요즘 믿을 수가 없다.)
a) is
b) was
c) be
d) been

정답 **d)**

2. **Choose the correct one for the blank.**
(빈칸에 맞는 표현을 고르시오.)

They are _______ the weather temperatures around the world.
(그것들은 전세계 기후에 영향을 끼친다.)

a) affecting
b) affects
c) effect
d) effects

정답 **a)**

3. **Choose the one which is not appropriate for the blank.**
(빈칸에 적절하지 않은 것을 고르시오)

I ________ you why it is so changeable.

a) am asking
b) ask
c) asks
d) have been asking

정답 **c)**

4. **Choose the correct one for the blank.**
(빈칸에 맞는 표현을 고르시오.)

Butterfly effect theory was _______ by an American meteorologist.
(나비 효과 이론은 미국의 기상학자에 의해 만들어졌다.)

a) creation
b) creates
c) creator
d) created

정답 **d)**

Review 15-2 B

1. **Choose the correct one for the blank.**
(빈칸에 맞는 표현을 고르시오.)

The average seawater temperature ______ around 1 degree in a decade.
(평균 해수면의 온도는 10년에 1도 정도 증가했다.)

a) increasable
b) incredible
c) increasing
d) increased

정답 **d)**

2. **Choose the correct one for the blank.**
(빈칸에 맞는 표현을 고르시오.)

The weather temperature has been _____ the rise.
(기온이 상승해왔다.)

a) to
b) on
c) with
d) within

정답 **b)**

3. **Choose the one which is not appropriate for the blank.**
(빈칸에 적절하지 않은 것을 고르시오)

The greenhouse effect is a ________ problem.

a) dreadful
b) disastrous
c) beneficial
d) serious

정답 **c)**

4. **Choose the correct one for the blank.**
(빈칸에 맞는 표현을 고르시오.)

He must _____ a Mr. Know-It-All.
(그는 만물박사임에 틀림없다.)

a) are
b) is
c) was
d) be

정답 **d)**

저자 약력

조동인

외국어대학교 영어과 학사 졸업

뉴욕주립대 석사

외국어대학교 문학 박사

현, 인하공업전문대학 어학교양학부 부교수